C000296563

Isaiah

TEACHING CHRIST IN ALL OF SCRIPTURE

Head, Heart, Hand Bible Studies

- Ezra and Nehemiah — *The Good Hand of Our God Is upon Us*
- Isaiah — *The Holy One of Israel*
- Romans — *The Gospel of God for Obedience to the Faith*
- 1 Peter, 2 Peter, and Jude — *Steadfast in the Faith*

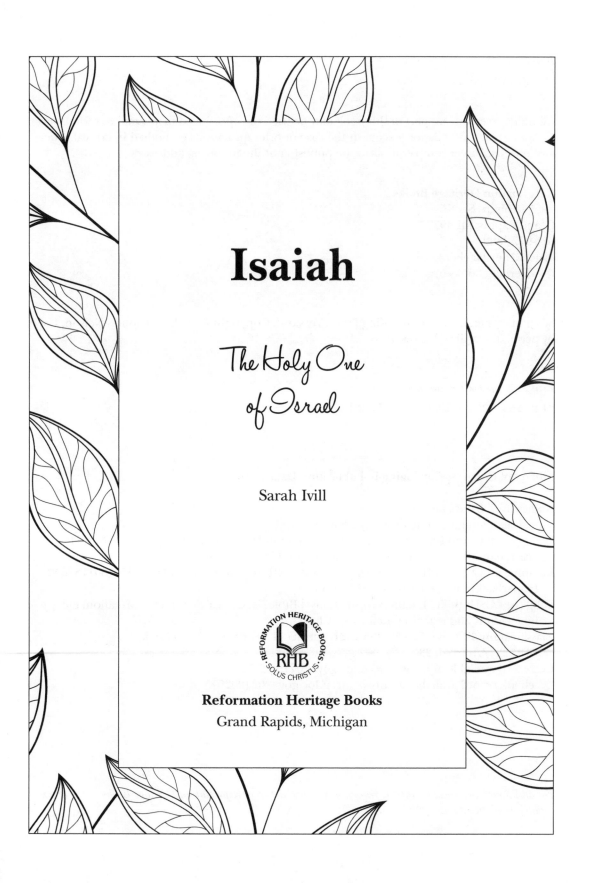

Isaiah

The Holy One of Israel

Sarah Ivill

Reformation Heritage Books
Grand Rapids, Michigan

Isaiah
© 2021 by Sarah Ivill

All rights reserved. No part of this book may be used or reproduced in any manner whatsoever without written permission except in the case of brief quotations embodied in critical articles and reviews. Direct your requests to the publisher at the following addresses:

Reformation Heritage Books
2965 Leonard St. NE
Grand Rapids, MI 49525
616-977-0889
orders@heritagebooks.org
www.heritagebooks.org

Scripture taken from the New King James Version®. Copyright © 1982 by Thomas Nelson. Used by permission. All rights reserved.

Printed in the United States of America
21 22 23 24 25 26/10 9 8 7 6 5 4 3 2 1

Library of Congress Cataloging-in-Publication Data

Names: Ivill, Sarah, author.
Title: Isaiah : the holy one of Israel / Sarah Ivill.
Description: Grand Rapids, Michigan : Reformation Heritage Books, [2021] | Series: Head, heart, hand Bible studies | Includes bibliographical references.
Identifiers: LCCN 2021002574 (print) | LCCN 2021002575 (ebook) | ISBN 9781601788542 (paperback) | ISBN 9781601788559 (epub)
Subjects: LCSH: Bible. Isaiah–Introductions. | Bible. Isaiah–Criticism, interpretation, etc. | Bible–Study and teaching–Reformed Church.
Classification: LCC BS1515.55 .I95 2021 (print) | LCC BS1515.55 (ebook) | DDC 224/.1061–dc23
LC record available at https://lccn.loc.gov/2021002574
LC ebook record available at https://lccn.loc.gov/2021002575

For additional Reformed literature, request a free book list from Reformation Heritage Books at the above regular or email address.

To the Lord my God,
The Holy One of Israel, my Savior,
Who will not let the rivers overflow me
Or the flame scorch me
And who will bring His daughters from the ends of the earth—
Everyone who is called by His name
Whom He has created for His glory
Whom He has formed and made
                    —from ISAIAH 43:2–3, 6–7

Contents

A Note from Sarah

Many women today are drowning in despair, flailing their arms in futility, and sinking in seas of sin and suffering. They reach out to false, futile saviors, clinging to things or relationships that are as capable of saving them as sticks floating in the sea and the wind that crashes with each wave. This is tragic, especially because the lifeboat that could secure them to the heaviest anchor is right in front of them. But they continue to try to save themselves, shirking the secure way.

Perhaps no one has told them that the lifeboat, the Word of God, is their very life because it reveals Jesus Christ, the anchor of their souls and the One to whom all Scripture points. Only as women are steeped in the Scriptures that point them to the Savior will they swim in hope, surf waves in security, and stand on shore anchored to the truth.

Let us return to being women of one Book above all others. If you have time to read only one book, make it Scripture. Then, if you have time to read more, you will be well trained to tell the difference between what merely tickles your ears and what mightily transforms your heart.

My love for teaching the Bible was inspired by my hunger to study it. Longing for the "meat" of God's Word and finding it lacking in so many churches today, I enrolled in Bible Study Fellowship after graduating from high school. It was there that I realized my desire to attend seminary and was influenced and encouraged by a strong, godly woman and mentor in my life to attend Dallas Theological Seminary (DTS). During this time I was leading women through in-depth Bible studies and caught a glimpse of how much women desired to be fed the depth of God's Word. This encouraged me even further to receive an education that would best prepare me to deliver God's Word to women who hungered for the truth.

After graduating with my master of theology from DTS, I took a position as assistant director of women's ministry at a large church where I served under a woman who shared my passion to teach the "meat" of God's Word. Within the year, I had assumed the role of director and delved into teaching the Bible in an expository and applicable manner. After three years I resigned in order to stay home with my first child. During those years at home, the Lord used my experience in seminary and ministry to lead me back to my roots and fully embrace Reformed theology. Raised for the first half of my childhood in conservative Presbyterian churches, I had been grounded in the Reformed faith and catechisms from an early age. But from middle school on, I was not in Reformed churches. The question in my twenties then became, What do I really believe?

One of the first steps on my journey was contacting a Reformed seminary and asking for a list of books covering everything I had missed by not attending a Reformed seminary. That began my reading of some of the most renowned Reformed theologians in the world. It was during those days that the question of what I really believed was finally answered, and I began teaching women based on my understanding of Reformed theology. In fact, that is how my first Bible study came to be written. I had the incredible privilege of teaching that first study to a wonderful group of women for a morning Bible study at our Presbyterian Church in America (PCA) church. And it was from their encouragement and exhortation that I submitted the study for publication.

I want to encourage you as you embark on the study of Isaiah. As you read, ponder what the Bible has to say about the depth of our sin and the judgment we deserve, and rejoice at the wonders of grace and salvation. In every chapter keep your eyes on Jesus, the one to whom all Scripture points, and worship Him for the work of salvation that He has accomplished for you through the power of the Holy Spirit, to the glory of God the Father. *Soli Deo gloria!*

Acknowledgments

I wish to thank those in my life who have been a part of this writing process.

Thank you to Reformation Heritage Books, especially Jay Collier for his interest in this project, Annette Gysen for her excellent editorial work, and Dr. Beeke for reviewing the manuscript.

Thank you to the pastors of Christ Covenant Church (PCA) for faithfully proclaiming the word of God each week. I especially want to thank the women (you know who you are!) who have encouraged me to keep writing Bible studies and have faithfully prayed for me.

Thank you to the men and women of Dallas Theological Seminary who taught me what it means to be a gracious student of Scripture and who instilled in me the importance of expository teaching and the love of God's word.

Thank you to Westminster Theological Seminary as well as to Reformed Theological Seminary and the professors who have served there. The many books that the professors have written and recommended as well as the many online class lectures and chapel messages have been of tremendous benefit to me. They have taught me what it means to see Christ in all of Scripture and to understand more deeply the history of redemption and the beautiful truths of Reformed theology.

Thank you to my dad and mom, David and Judy Gelaude, who have always supported me in my love of the Word and encouraged me to do that which the Lord has called me to do. I love you both more than words can express.

Thank you to my husband, Charles, who has always given me his love, support, and encouragement in the writing process and in what the Lord has called me to do.

And thank you to my children—Caleb, Hannah, Daniel, and Lydia—whose smiles, hugs, and prayers are a constant source of encouragement to me as I pray for the next generation of believers to love the Lord and His word with all their hearts and minds.

Finally, thank you to my heavenly Father, to my Lord and Savior Jesus Christ, and to the Spirit, who helps me in my weakness. To the triune God be the glory for what He has done through me, a broken vessel and a flawed instrument, yet one that is in the grip of His mighty and gracious hand.

Introduction to This Study

It is my sincere hope that you are excited about studying Scripture, particularly the book of Isaiah. It is also my sincere desire that this study will help fuel your excitement. In this introduction I have provided three resources that I hope will prove beneficial to you. First, I have provided an overview of how to use this Bible study. Feel free to adapt my suggestions for the context in which you will be using this study. I want this study to be a help to you, not a hindrance!

Second, I have provided an overview of the history of redemption and revelation. When we study Scripture, it is sometimes easy to get so focused on the original context that we forget to pull back and study a passage with regard to its redemptive-historical context (which considers the question of where we are in salvation history). I hope this overview gives you a sense of the overarching story of Scripture.

Finally, I have provided an overview of what it means to study Christ in all of Scripture. Often, people struggle with how to teach the Old Testament in a Christ-centered way. Many times the book of Isaiah is taught in a legalistic or moralistic way, focusing more on what we are to do than on what Christ has already done for us. It is crucial we connect the passages to Christ first so that we understand our salvation is by grace alone through faith alone.

How to Use This Bible Study

This study is organized into four main parts:

(1) *Purpose*: This brief section introduces you to the passage you will be studying and is meant to guide you into how the lesson applies to your head (knowledge about God), your heart (affection for God), and your hands (service for God). Although it is brief, this is a significant section to read since it tells you in a nutshell what the lesson is all about, giving you the big picture before studying the finer details.

(2) *Personal Study*: This section of questions is meant to help you dig deeply into God's Word so that you might be equipped to worship God, work for His kingdom purposes, and witness for Him to a watching world. To assist you in your study, you may want to have a good study Bible and concordance close at hand. I would encourage

you not to get overwhelmed by the questions or think you have to answer every one of them, but to relax and enjoy the study of God's Word.

(3) *Putting It All Together.* This section is meant to help answer any lingering questions you may still have after your personal study time and assist you in tying things together from the lesson questions. It will prove helpful in cementing in your mind everything you've previously studied and will better prepare you to process things together with your Bible study group.

(4) *Processing It Together.* This section of questions is meant to help you study the Bible in the context of community, sharing what you have learned together so that you might sharpen one another, encourage one another, and pray for one another. Group leaders: Ideally, the women have worked through the previous three sections before coming together as a group. Your first gathering might be a time of fellowship and a discussion of the introduction to the book. Then you can assign the ladies the homework for the first lesson. Encourage them to read the purpose, work through the personal study questions, and read through "Putting It All Together." Remind them to relax and enjoy the study, encouraging them to come to the group time regardless of whether their homework is complete. You may want to star certain questions from your personal study that you want to cover in the group time, as well as highlight any sections from "Putting It All Together" to discuss. I would recommend reviewing the "Purpose" at the beginning of your group time as well. Don't forget to begin and end with prayer and to foster a warm and inviting environment where women can grow together in thinking biblically, being grounded in the truth, and living covenantally, being anchored in the covenant community.

Now that we have taken a look at how this study is organized, let's turn our attention to the big story of the Bible so that we might have a better grasp of the bigger context in which Isaiah fits.

An Overview of the History of Redemption and Revelation

God has chosen to enter into a covenant relationship with His people. He is the covenant King; we are the covenant servants. As our covenant King, He acts in history, bringing about both His word and His works and providentially ensures that the faith is passed from generation to generation. As His covenant servants, we are to obey His word.

It is only in Christ that the covenant King and the covenant servants meet. Christ is both the Lord of the covenant and the Servant of the covenant. He has come as Lord to extend grace and mercy to God's rebellious servants, and He has come as the Servant of the covenant to perfectly fulfill what God's people could never do, thus bringing blessing to all those who place their faith in Him.

Amazingly, our covenant King has chosen to dwell among His people. Throughout redemptive history we see a progression of God dwelling with His people. First, we observe Him dwelling with Adam and Eve in the garden. Then we see Him meet with His people in the tabernacle and then the temple and dwell with them there. But the climax is when Jesus came to earth and tabernacled among us, fulfilling God's promise, "I will take you as My people, and I will be your God" (Ex. 6:7). When Christ returns He will consummately fulfill this promise as we dwell with the triune God in the new heaven and the new earth forever (Rev. 21:3).

If we are to understand the overarching story of Scripture, we need to recognize the different covenants in the history of redemption: the covenant of redemption, the covenant of works, and the covenant of grace. What theologians call the *covenant of redemption* is described in Ephesians 1:4, which teaches us that God the Father chose us in Christ "before the foundation of the world, that we should be holy and without blame before Him." The Father has appointed our redemption, the Son has accomplished it, and the Holy Spirit applies it.

In Genesis 1–2 we learn of God's covenant with Adam before the fall. This covenant established a relationship between the Creator and the creature that involved *worship* (keeping the Sabbath day holy), *work* (ruling and multiplying), *woman* (marriage and procreation), and the *word of God* (God gave Adam a command when He put him in the garden of Eden to work it and keep it. He could eat of any tree in the garden except one, the tree of the knowledge of good and evil. God told Adam that if he ate of that tree he would die; if he obeyed, he would live). Theologians refer to this prefall covenant with Adam as the *covenant of works*, the *covenant of life*, or the *covenant of creation*.

Tragically, Adam failed to obey, and all mankind fell with him in this first sin. But God sounds a note of grace in Genesis 3:15: death will not have the final word. God promises that He will put enmity between the serpent and the woman, between the serpent's offspring and the woman's offspring. The woman's offspring would bruise the serpent's head, and the serpent would bruise His heel. This is the gospel in seed form. Ultimately, the woman's offspring is Christ. Christ defeated sin and death on the cross, triumphing over all His enemies.

Along with God's blessed promise to the woman that she would continue to produce *seed*, or offspring, the greatest of which is Christ, He also told her that she would experience the curse of *sorrow* with regard to children and the curse of *struggle* with regard to her husband.

God spoke a word to Adam also. He promised the man that he would receive the blessing of *sustenance*. But he would also experience the curse of *sweaty toil* and the *separation of soul and body* in death. Theologians call this postfall covenant the *covenant of grace*. The Westminster Larger Catechism 31 states, "The covenant of grace was made with Christ as the second Adam, and in him with all the elect as his seed." Titus 3:4–7 provides a good summary of this covenant: "But when the kindness and the love of God our Savior toward man appeared, not by works of righteousness which we have done, but according to His mercy He saved us, through the washing of regeneration and renewing of the Holy Spirit, whom He poured out on us abundantly through

Jesus Christ our Savior, that having been justified by His grace we should become heirs according to the hope of eternal life." The covenant of grace includes God's post-fall covenant with Adam (Gen. 3:15), Noah (Gen. 6:17–22; 8:20–22; 9:1–17), Abraham (Gen. 12:1–3; 15:1–21; 17:1–2), Moses (Exodus 19–24 and Deuteronomy), and David (2 Samuel 7), as well as the new covenant, all of which are fulfilled in Jesus Christ (Jer. 31:31–34). Let's take a closer look now at each of these covenants, as well as some other important events that were occurring in redemptive history, so that we have a better grasp of the story of salvation.

After the note of the gospel of grace is sounded to Adam and Eve in Genesis 3:15, we learn of God's covenant with Noah recorded in Genesis 9. The Lord promises that as long as the earth remains, seedtime and harvest, cold and heat, summer and winter, and day and night will continue. This is amazing grace, for it promises that there will be an earth on which the history of salvation will unfold. Just think if there had been no day for Jesus to be born in Bethlehem or to die on the cross!

God's covenant with Noah also promises that though the righteous will be saved, the wicked will be judged, a theme that is predominant all through Scripture. God's original purposes of worship, work, and woman in the prefall covenant with Adam are renewed in the context of the history of redemption. God's covenant with Noah can be summarized by the following: God's *glorious grace* alongside His *glorious justice*; the *genealogical aspect* of the covenant (God will deal with families, not just individuals); the *goodness* of life; and the *general grace* extended to all mankind, including the universe. The sign of this covenant, the rainbow, is most appropriate, then, as it shines God's grace in the midst of the cloudy storm of judgment.

In Genesis 12, 15, 17, and 22, we learn of God's covenant with Abraham, which is later renewed with Isaac and Jacob. First, God promises His *presence.* The crux of the covenant of grace can be summed up in one phrase, "I will walk among you and be your God, and you shall be My people" (Lev. 26:12). Second, God promises Abraham a *people*; God would make him a great nation. Third, God promises Abraham a *possession*; He would give His people the land of Canaan. Fourth, God promises Abraham that he has a bigger *purpose* than he could ever imagine. The nation that came through his seed was to point others to the Lord so that all the families of the earth would be blessed.

In Exodus, we learn of God's covenant with Moses, the mediator of the law God gave to Israel, which can be summarily comprehended in the Ten Commandments. This is the beginning of the theocratic nation of Israel.[1] God brought His people out of slavery in Egypt and into a relationship with Him as servants of the Holy God. As such, they were to be a kingdom of priests and a holy nation (Ex. 19:6). We learn in both Leviticus 26 and Deuteronomy 28 that if they were obedient, they would receive blessings (Lev. 26:1–13; Deut. 28:1–14), but if they were disobedient, they would receive

---

1. By a theocratic nation, I mean that Israel's earthly kings, priests, and prophets recognized God as the true King, and as such served to interpret and enforce His laws for the people.

curses (Lev. 26:14–46; Deut. 28:15–68). One of these curses, the greatest, was exile from the land. But even toward the end of Deuteronomy, we see that God made provision for restoration after the exile, which involved the new covenant (Deut. 30:1–10; see also Jer. 31:31–34; Ezek. 37:21, 26).

In fact, Deuteronomy 28–30 is the "CliffsNotes" version of the rest of the Old Testament. First comes blessing, climaxing in the reign of King Solomon (1 Kings 8:24). Then come curses, ultimately resulting in exile from the land (2 Chron. 36:17–21). All the prophets refer to the covenant blessings and curses as they prophesy to Israel and Judah, giving them messages of judgment as well as holding out the hope of blessing. Though the prophets declare that exile is inevitable, they also declare God's faithfulness to His covenant, keeping the promise of the new covenant before them (Deut. 30:1–10; Jer. 31:31–34; Ezek. 37:21, 26).

After Moses died, the Lord raised up Joshua to lead the people into the promised land, which was the place where God would dwell with His people in the temple. Up to this point in redemptive history, the garden of Eden and the tabernacle had been the places where the Lord had temporarily dwelt with His people. The entire book of Joshua centers on the entry into and conquest of the land.

But then Joshua died, and in the book of Judges we see that the people failed to conquer the land as they should have. Instead, they did what was right in their own eyes because there was no king in Israel. The books of Judges and Ruth anticipate the beginning of the monarchy in Israel with King Saul and King David.

In 2 Samuel 7, God makes a covenant with David concerning an eternal kingdom with an eternal Davidic king. First, God promises David a *position*, taking him from being a shepherd of sheep to making him a shepherd king over his people with a great name. Second, God promises David a *place*. Israel would be planted in the land of Canaan. Third, God promises David *peace*. In their own place, Israel would have rest from their enemies. Finally, God promises David *progeny*. The Lord would raise up David's offspring and establish his kingdom forever.

The period of the monarchy climaxes in King Solomon, when the promises are fulfilled in Solomon's prayer of dedication (1 Kings 8:24). Sadly, it didn't take long (within Solomon's reign) for the monarchy to take a turn for the worse (1 Kings 11). Following Solomon's death, the country actually divided into the Northern Kingdom (Israel) and the Southern Kingdom (Judah) in 931 BC (1 Kings 12:16–24).

Elijah and Elisha preached to the Northern Kingdom during this time. Although there were a few good kings, the majority of kings in both Israel and Judah did evil in the sight of the Lord and led the people into rebellion as well. In His grace and mercy, God raised up prophets during this time to prophesy to the people of coming judgment so that they would turn and repent of their wicked ways. Hosea and Amos preached to the Northern Kingdom, while Isaiah and Micah preached to the Southern Kingdom. Joel, Obadiah, and Jonah also preached their messages during this time.

Tragically, the Northern Kingdom did not listen and was taken into captivity by the Assyrians in 722 BC.

A little over one hundred years later, the same thing happened to the Southern Kingdom, except it was the Babylonians who took them into captivity. This involved three different deportations in 605, 597, and 586 BC. In the second of these deportations, Jehoiachin, the last true Davidic king on the throne, was taken, along with the royal family and all the leading classes in Israel, to Babylon. God's promises seemed to be thwarted.

But again, in God's mercy, He raised up both Daniel and Ezekiel to prophesy to the people during the exile (Jeremiah was still prophesying during this time as well). Daniel and Ezekiel spoke messages of both judgment and restoration to the exiles. God would still be faithful to His covenant promise; He would be their God, and they would be His people. Both Jeremiah and Ezekiel spoke of the promised new covenant (Jer. 31:31–34; Ezek. 37:21, 26), inaugurated by Christ during the last Passover (which was also the first Lord's Supper) with His disciples before His death.

The new covenant involved seven different promises. First, God promised His people would *return* to the land of promise. Second, God promised a *restoration of the land.* Third, God promised a *realization* of *each of His previous promises* to Adam, Noah, Abraham, Moses, and David. Fourth, God promised a *renewed heart.* Fifth, God promised the *removal of sin.* Sixth, God promised a *reunion of Israel and Judah under one ruler,* Jesus Christ. Finally, God promised the *realization of redemption* (this was the final covenant, and, as such, it secured redemption).

Following the exile, God raised up the prophets Haggai, Zechariah, and Malachi to continue speaking to His people. Though there is a small fulfillment of a restored temple, people, and land under the leadership of Zerubbabel, Ezra, and Nehemiah, the promises of God could not be completely fulfilled until Jesus Christ came. As Paul so eloquently says, "All the promises of God in Him are Yes, and in Him Amen, to the glory of God through us" (2 Cor. 1:20).

The Gospels record for us the amazing truth of the incarnation. Jesus came to earth as a baby, lived a life of perfect obedience, died for the sins of God's people, was raised as the firstfruits of the resurrection, and ascended to the Father. Acts 2 records that the Holy Spirit was sent on the day of Pentecost to renew the church and establish it by His power.

The new age was inaugurated through Christ and His church, but it awaits its consummation until Christ returns to bring the old age to a complete end with the final judgment and usher in the new heaven and the new earth. In the meantime, the church is to fulfill the Great Commission: "And Jesus came and spoke to them, saying, 'All authority has been given to Me in heaven and on earth. Go therefore and make disciples of all the nations, baptizing them in the name of the Father and of the Son and of the Holy Spirit, teaching them to observe all things that I have commanded you; and lo, I am with you always, even to the end of the age.' Amen" (Matt. 28:18–20; see also Luke 24:47–49).

As we study any passage of Scripture, it is important for us to keep this overview of the history of redemption and revelation in mind. After studying the original context of the passage, we must ask the question, How does this text relate to the history of redemption? In other words, where is it in progressive, redemptive history? Then we must ask, How does this text relate to the climax of redemptive history—the life, death, resurrection, and ascension of our Lord and Savior Jesus Christ? The latter question leads us to the next section we need to consider in order to teach Christ in all of Scripture.

A Christ-Centered Interpretation of Isaiah

The story of Jesus begins in the Old Testament in the opening chapters of Genesis with the account of creation. As the apostle John so eloquently says, "In the beginning was the Word, and the Word was with God, and the Word was God. He was in the beginning with God. All things were made through Him, and without Him nothing was made that was made. In Him was life, and the life was the light of men. And the light shines in the darkness, and the darkness did not comprehend it" (John 1:1–5). Paul echoes this truth in Colossians 1:15–17: "He is the image of the invisible God, the first-born over all creation. For by Him all things were created that are in heaven and that are on earth, visible and invisible, whether thrones or dominions or principalities or powers. All things were created through Him and for Him. And He is before all things, and in Him all things consist."

Matthew, like John, doesn't begin his gospel account with the birth of Jesus; rather, he opens with the genealogy of Jesus Christ, reaching all the way back through the Old Testament to Abraham. In chapter 3 of his gospel, Luke goes back even further, tracing the story of Jesus all the way to Adam, the son of God. Paul too traces the story of Jesus back to Adam when he says, "And so it is written, 'The first man Adam became a living being.' The last Adam became a life-giving spirit" (1 Cor. 15:45). Even before the fall, the first man Adam pointed forward to the greater and final Adam, Jesus Christ. Luke closes his gospel with Jesus's own account of His story, so since we are learning about Him from Him, we should pay close attention as we read His words in Luke 24.

Two disciples were trying to put the story of Jesus together. They had been in Jerusalem and witnessed the events at the end of Jesus's life. They had seven long miles to try to figure it out as they journeyed from Jerusalem to Emmaus, but they couldn't understand. They were deeply distressed. Their hope had been deflated. They thought that He was the one to redeem Israel, but instead He was crucified and buried. Indeed, the tomb was empty, but Jesus was nowhere to be seen.

Note carefully what Jesus says to them: "'O foolish ones, and slow of heart to believe in all that the prophets have spoken! Ought not the Christ to have suffered these things and to enter into His glory?' And beginning at Moses and all the

Prophets, He expounded to them in all the Scriptures the things concerning Himself" (Luke 24:25–27).

Wouldn't you have liked to walk those seven miles with the three of them? It was the greatest walk those disciples would have in their entire lives as the Master Teacher told His own story, beginning in Genesis and moving all the way through the Prophets. It was the privilege of not only these two Emmaus disciples to hear Jesus tell His story but also the disciples who had been with Him during His earthly ministry. Luke tells us later in the same chapter that Jesus opened their minds to understand the Scriptures, everything written about Him in the Law of Moses and the Prophets and the Psalms. These things had to be fulfilled, and Jesus was telling them that He was the fulfillment (Luke 24:44–47).

He is the second Adam, who did not sin but was obedient to death on the cross. He is the Seed of the woman, who crushed the serpent's head (Gen. 3:15). He is the final Noah, who saved His people through the cross (Eph. 2:16). He is the final Abraham, in whom all the families of the earth are blessed (Acts 2:38–39; 3:25–26; Gal. 3:13–14, 29). He is the final Isaac, who was sacrificed for our sin. He is the final Passover Lamb (Ex. 12:13). He is the final sacrifice, whose blood atoned for our sins (Lev. 16:14–16). He is the final and perfect priest, who is greater than Aaron (Heb. 9:11–12). He is the true Israel, who was tested and tried in the wilderness and obeyed (Matt. 4:1–11). He is the one lifted up to deliver sinners from death (Num. 21:9). He is the Prophet greater than Moses (Deut. 18:15–22). He is the one who gives grace to covenant breakers (Deut. 27:1–26). He is the ark of the covenant and the blood on the mercy seat (Heb. 9:1–14). He is the true bread of life and the light of the world on the golden lampstand (John 6:48, 51; 8:12). He is the Commander of the army of the Lord (Josh. 5:14). He is the final Judge, who never fell into sin but delivered His people by taking their judgment for them (2 Cor. 5:21). He is the final kinsman-redeemer greater than Boaz (Ruth 3:12–13). He is the final Psalmist, who leads His people in praise to God (Heb. 2:12). He is the final Davidic King, who reigns in perfect justice and righteousness (John 18:37). He is the final Solomon, who not only is full of wisdom but is wisdom Himself (1 Cor. 1:30). He is the final Prophet, who suffered for His people and did so without opening His mouth in retaliation (Isaiah 53). And He is the Great Shepherd of the sheep (Ezek. 34:11–24).

Peter is proof that Jesus opened His disciples' minds to understand that day, for in Acts 2 we read his sermon, which he begins by citing David's words in Psalm 16:8–11 and ends by citing his words in Psalm 110:1. He speaks these words in between:

> Men and brethren, let me speak freely to you of the patriarch David, that he is both dead and buried, and his tomb is with us to this day. Therefore, being a prophet, and knowing that God had sworn with an oath to him that of the fruit of his body, according to the flesh, He would raise up the Christ to sit on his throne, he, foreseeing this, spoke concerning the resurrection of the Christ, that His soul was not left in

Hades, nor did His flesh see corruption. This Jesus God has raised up, of which we are all witnesses. Therefore being exalted to the right hand of God, and having received from the Father the promise of the Holy Spirit, He poured out this which you now see and hear. (Acts 2:29–33)

We cannot tell the story of Jesus in any way we please. We must learn from Jesus Himself and tell the story beginning with Genesis through Deuteronomy, moving through the Prophets and the Psalms, and then the New Testament Gospels and Letters, closing with Revelation, where the end of the story is told: "Now I saw a new heaven and a new earth, for the first heaven and the first earth had passed away" (Rev. 21:1). The end of the story isn't really the end, for we will spend an eternity worshiping Him "who is and who was and who is to come,... Jesus Christ, the faithful witness, the firstborn from the dead, and the ruler over the kings of the earth," the One who loves us and has freed us from our sins by His blood and "has made us kings and priests to His God and Father" (Rev. 1:4–6).

We have looked at some key texts, so now let's look at some key phrases for identifying the continuity between the Old and New Testaments. We might say that we go from Old Testament promise to New Testament fulfillment, or from Old Testament problem (sinners in need of a Savior) to New Testament solution (the Savior comes), or from Old Testament anticipation to New Testament realization, but not just a realization—a far-surpassing realization. For example, Jesus Christ is not just a greater Moses, Samson, prophet, priest, or king, but the greatest and final Moses, Samson, prophet, priest, and king. Furthermore, the Lord of history designs historical persons, offices, institutions, and events to foreshadow the full redemption to come. Thus, He foreshadows His great work of redemption in both words and works (events).[2]

The climax in all of Scripture is the gospel—the life, death, resurrection, and ascension of Jesus Christ. All the Old Testament writers look toward this climax. All the New Testament writers look both back to this climax and forward to the consummation of the kingdom, Christ's second coming, which was inaugurated at His first coming. There are really four main questions, then, when we are studying Scripture: (1) What is the original context of this passage? (2) Where are we in the history of redemption in this text? (3) How does this text relate to the gospel? (4) How do I apply this text to my life right now in light of where I am in redemptive history?

These questions keep us from a legalistic reading of the text ("Do this, and you will live"), a moralistic reading of the text ("Be a good person, and you will be saved"), a therapeutic reading of the text ("I'm good, you're good, God is good, everything is okay"), and an allegorical reading of the text ("I'm going to make this text refer to Christ no matter what interpretive principles I have to break!"). Instead, we will be women who glean a Christ-centered message.

---

2. Dennis Johnson, *Him We Proclaim: Preaching Christ from All the Scriptures* (Phillipsburg, N.J.: P&R, 2007), 225–26.

Introduction to Isaiah

A flurry of words swirls around us these days. Through various channels of media, especially social media, people readily voice their opinions with little or no thought of the ramifications. Imagine, if you can, someone on the news, or on their social media platform, saying,

> Woe is me, for I am undone!
> Because I am a [woman] of unclean lips,
> And I dwell in the midst of a people of unclean lips;
> For my eyes have seen the King,
> The LORD of hosts. (Isa. 6:5)

The church of today needs to call God's people to holiness in a world that is unclean. Studying the book of Isaiah is a good place to start. Isaiah uses the word *holy* to describe the Lord God more than all the other Old Testament books combined.[1] This Holy God calls His people to holiness, and through His King, Servant, and Conqueror, all fulfilled in Jesus Christ, ensures that their sins are atoned for and their hearts empowered to live for Him.

The Author, Date, and Historical Background of Isaiah

The divine author of Scripture is God Himself: "All Scripture is given by inspiration of God, and is profitable for doctrine, for reproof, for correction, for instruction in righteousness, that the man of God may be complete, thoroughly equipped for every good work" (2 Tim. 3:16–17). But the Holy Spirit used human authors to speak and write the word of God (2 Peter 1:21).

---

1. J. Alec Motyer, *The Prophecy of Isaiah: An Introduction and Commentary* (Downers Grove, Ill.: IVP Academic, 1993), 19.

Isaiah the son of Amoz is the author of all sixty-six chapters of this glorious, gospel-centered book. The New Testament makes this clear by ascribing passages from chapters 1–39 and 40–66 to Isaiah (see Matt. 3:3; 4:14; 8:17; 12:17; 13:14; 15:7; John 1:23; 12:38–41; Acts 8:28–30; 28:25; Rom. 9:27–29; 10:16–20; 15:12). Isaiah served as God's prophet to Judah from the time of King Uzziah's death (740/739 BC) through the reigns of Jotham (750–735 BC), Ahaz (735–715 BC), and Hezekiah (716/15–687/86 BC).[2] During Isaiah's ministry there were four Assyrian kings who threatened the Northern Kingdom of Israel and the Southern Kingdom of Judah, so both Israel and Judah were tempted to trust in alliances with other nations instead of in the Lord God. Two main crises presented themselves to Judah during Isaiah's ministry. The first was during the reign of King Ahaz, when the Northern Kingdom waged war on Jerusalem and besieged Ahaz but couldn't conquer him (2 Kings 16:5). Foolishly, Ahaz made an alliance with Assyria for protection against the Northern Kingdom instead of trusting in the Lord (2 Kings 16:6–9). It was also during King Ahaz's reign that the Northern Kingdom went into exile at the hand of the Assyrians in 722 BC. The second crisis came during King Hezekiah's reign when an opportunity for him to rebel against Assyria arose. Hezekiah was presented with offers from both Egypt and Babylon for an alliance against Assyria. Foolishly, like his father, Ahaz, Hezekiah allied with these powers and faced the inevitable consequences of trusting in kings instead of the King of kings.[3]

It is important to remember that Isaiah began prophesying in 740 BC, which was eighteen years before the Northern Kingdom went into exile in 722 BC and 135 years before the first deportation of the Southern Kingdom at the hand of the Babylonians in 605 BC. Since Isaiah lived and prophesied during the Northern Kingdom's exile, that event shaped his ministry to the Southern Kingdom. In the first thirty-seven chapters, Isaiah holds before his audience the hope of the Davidic king who is not just the ruler of Israel and Judah but of the whole world. It is through this king that grace is found and hope abounds. In chapters 38–55 the songs of the Suffering Servant provide comfort for a people who will be in exile in the near or distant future (Isaiah and his contemporaries didn't know when the Babylonian exile would occur). In chapters 56–66 Isaiah presents a breathtaking picture of the conquering King and His kingdom in order to encourage God's people living during the dark days of the Assyrians and ultimately God's people of all times surrounded by the darkness of this world, to keep an eternal perspective by looking in hope to the new creation.

The Purpose of Isaiah
During the dark days of the looming Assyrian threat over both Israel and Judah, when Israel and Judah were turning from God to trust in military, political, or religious powers, Isaiah stepped onto the scene to remind God's people that God's promises to Abraham, in which all the families of the earth would be blessed through Israel (Gen.

---

2. Motyer, *Prophecy of Isaiah*, 18.
3. Motyer, *Prophecy of Isaiah*, 19–21.

12:1–3), and His promises to David, in which there would never cease to be a Davidic king on the throne (2 Sam. 7:1–17), were still firmly in place and would be for all time.

The purpose of Isaiah becomes even clearer when we take a look at some key verses from the book:

- Alas, sinful nation…. / They have provoked to anger / the Holy One of Israel. (1:4)

- Therefore my people have gone into captivity, / because they have no knowledge. (5:13)

- Woe is me, for I am undone!
  Because I am a man of unclean lips,
  And I dwell in the midst of a people of unclean lips;
  For my eyes have seen the King,
  The LORD of hosts. (6:5)

- If you will not believe, / surely you shall not be established. (7:9)

- There shall come forth a Rod from the stem of Jesse,
  And a Branch shall grow out of his roots.
  The Spirit of the LORD shall rest upon Him. (11:1–2)

- Come near, you nations, to hear…. / For the indignation of the LORD is against all nations. (34:1–2)

- Then the eyes of the blind shall be opened, / and the ears of the deaf shall be unstopped. (35:5)

- For out of Jerusalem shall go a remnant,
  And those who escape from Mount Zion.
  The zeal of the LORD of hosts will do this. (37:32)

- "Comfort, yes, comfort My people!" / says your God. (40:1)

- Behold! My Servant whom I uphold,
  My Elect One in whom My soul delights!
  I have put my Spirit upon Him;
  He will bring forth justice to the Gentiles. (42:1)

- I will also give You as a light to the Gentiles, / that You should be My salvation to the ends of the earth. (49:6)

- For Zion's sake I will not hold My peace,
  And for Jerusalem's sake I will not rest,
  Until her righteousness goes forth as brightness,
  And her salvation as a lamp that burns. (62:1)

- For behold, I create new heavens and a new earth;
  And the former shall not be remembered or come to mind.
  But be glad and rejoice forever in what I create;
  For behold, I create Jerusalem as a rejoicing,
  And her people a joy. (65:17–18)

- But on this one will I look:
  On him who is poor and of a contrite spirit,
  And who trembles at My word. (66:2)

- For by fire and by His sword
  The LORD will judge all flesh;
  And the slain of the LORD shall be many. (66:16)

An Outline of Isaiah

Different and detailed outlines of Isaiah can be found in commentaries, but for this Bible study, I suggest the following:

> I. The Mighty Sovereign (chapters 1–37)
>
> II. The Mighty Servant (chapters 38–55)
>
> III. The Mighty Savior (chapters 56–66)[4]

Each lesson will further divide this broad outline into smaller parts, but for now, make note of these major divisions as you prepare to study Isaiah.

Over the next several weeks, you will have ample opportunity to come face-to-face with your sinfulness; your desperate need of a Savior; the holiness of God, the King of the nations; the atoning work of Jesus Christ; the call to carry the gospel to the nations; the hard-heartedness of people who embrace sin; and the glory that awaits us when Christ returns. Stop now and pray to prepare your heart for this study. This is the book the Lord used to convert the Ethiopian eunuch who was returning from Jerusalem and to whom Philip was sent to explain the good news about Jesus using Isaiah 53 (Acts 8:26–39). You too need to know how to explain the gospel according to Isaiah.

---

4. Motyer divides Isaiah into the Book of the King (1–37), the Book of the Servant (38–55), and the Book of the Anointed Conqueror (56–66). *Prophecy of Isaiah*, 13.

The Lord Confronts, Consoles, and Condemns

Isaiah 1–5

Purpose...

Head. What do I need to know from this passage in Scripture?

- The Lord confronts Judah's sin and condemns her for her idolatry. The only consolation is the coming branch of the Lord, which is ultimately Jesus Christ.

Heart. How does what I learn from this passage affect my internal relationship with the Lord?

- I am a sinner saved by grace alone and a kingdom disciple united to Christ, the beautiful and glorious one who sanctifies and beautifies me for Himself.

Hands. How does what I learn from this passage translate into action for God's kingdom?

- I will engage in corporate worship with my church family.
- I will pray for the gospel to be proclaimed boldly and clearly among the nations.
- I will teach my children and grandchildren, as well as covenant children in my church, to walk in the light of the Lord.
- I will help care for the poor and needy in my neighborhood, church, city, and beyond.
- I will recognize, record, and recall for the next generation all that the Lord has done for me.

Personal Study...

Pray. Ask that God will open up your heart and mind as you study His Word. This is His story of redemption that He has revealed to us, and the Holy Spirit is our teacher.

Ponder the Passage. Skim Isaiah. Then reread Isaiah 1–5.

- *Point.* What is the point of this passage? How does this relate to the point of the entire book?

- *People.* Who are the main people involved in this passage? What characterizes them?

- *Persons of the Trinity.* Where do you see God the Father, God the Son, and God the Holy Spirit in this passage?

- *Puzzling Parts.* Are there any parts of the passage that you don't quite understand or that seem interesting or confusing?

Put It in Perspective.

- *Place in Scripture.* What is the original context of this text? What is the redemptive-historical context—what has or hasn't happened in redemptive history at this point in Scripture? How does this text connect to Christ?

The following questions will help you if you got stuck on any of the previous questions, and they will help you dig a little deeper into the text, putting it all into perspective.

1. **1:1.** (a) What do you learn about Uzziah's (also called Azariah) reign in 2 Kings 15:1–7; Jotham's reign in 15:32–38; Ahaz's reign in 16:1–20; and Hezekiah's reign in 18:1–20:21?

   (b) What occurred in the Northern Kingdom of Israel during this period (see 2 Kings 18:9–12)?

   (c) Why didn't Assyria attack the Southern Kingdom of Judah (see 2 Kings 19:6–7, 15–19, 32–37)?

2. 1:2–9. (a) How is the Lord's relationship with Judah defined? What do you learn about His relationship with Israel in Exodus 4:22–23; 6:5–8; 19:4–6?

(b) How are the people of Judah described?

(c) How is the country described?

(d) Where do you see God's mercy in these verses?

(e) What do you learn about Sodom and Gomorrah in Genesis 19:1–29?

3. 1:10–20. (a) What had Judah's worship become?

(b) What did the Lord want from them, and how does this reflect His character?

(c) What is the note of grace the Lord sounds? How does this anticipate Romans 5:6–11?

4. 1:21–26. (a) Compare Judah's former condition with their condition described in these verses.

(b) What will the Lord do? How is this ultimately fulfilled in Revelation 21:1–22:5?

5. 1:27–31. (a) Contrast the righteous and the transgressors. What makes the difference?

(b) How do these verses anticipate the final judgment, in which believers will enter an eternity in the new heavens and the new earth and unbelievers will enter an eternity in hell?

6. 2:1–5. (a) Compare these verses with Micah 4:1–3. To what does Isaiah call Judah?

(b) How do these verses anticipate Christ (see John 1:1–5; 4:23; 8:12; Acts 2:1–13)?

(c) How do these verses anticipate Ephesians 5:8?

7. 2:6–22. (a) In light of Deuteronomy 16:21–17:7, why is the covenant Lord just in bringing judgment against Judah?

(b) How do these verses anticipate the Babylonian exile that the people of Judah would face beginning with the first deportation in 605 BC?

(c) How do these verses ultimately anticipate the final day of judgment (see Rev. 6:15–16)?

8. 3:1–4:1. (a) Skim Leviticus 26 and Deuteronomy 28. How do these chapters form the background for these verses?

(b) How do verses 10–11 anticipate Matthew 25:31–46?

9. 4:2–6. (a) What is the hope these verses radiate after the news in chapter 3?

(b) Who is the Branch (see Jer. 23:5–6)?

(c) How do these verses anticipate Luke 1:67–79 and Hebrews 12:18–24?

10. 5:1–7. (a) Using Psalm 80:8–15, explain who is meant by "my Well-beloved" and what is meant by "vineyard."

(b) Give examples from Scripture of the Beloved caring for the vineyard.

(c) How does this story reflect the strategy Nathan used when speaking with David about his sin (see 2 Sam. 12:1–14)?

(d) How do these verses anticipate Matthew 21:33–46?

11. 5:8–30. (a) The Lord points out several specific sins in these verses. How would you categorize them?

(b) Compared with the earlier chapters, specifically 1:9, 18–19, 26–27; 2:1–5; 3:10; 4:2–6, what is missing in this chapter?

(c) How do these verses reveal the need for a Redeemer?

(d) How do they anticipate Luke 11:42–52 and ultimately Revelation 19:11–16?

Principles and Points of Application

12. **1:1–31.** In these verses, what challenges you to evaluate whether your heart is motivating your worship? Are you going through the motions of corporate worship and personal devotions, or is your heart warm toward the things of God? Does your lifestyle reflect your profession of faith?

13. **2:1–22.** (a) In what ways are you proclaiming the gospel to the nations? What are some ways you can be more informed in your prayers for Christians working around the world to bring the gospel message to those around them in a fruitful and effective way?

    (b) What are the evidences that you are walking in the light of the Lord? In what ways are you teaching your children and grandchildren, as well as the covenant children in your church, to do so by God's grace?

    (c) In what ways are you tempted by materialism? How has "treasure" become an idol in your life?

    (d) In what areas of life do you fear man more than God? What is the challenge of Isaiah 2:22?

14. **3:1–4:1.** (a) How does a better grasp of the covenant curses help you appreciate even more the life and death of Jesus?

(b) How do you help care for the poor and needy in your neighborhood, church, city, and beyond?

(c) In what ways does the fleeting beauty of this world captivate you? What does Scripture say about beauty, and how do these verses challenge you (for example, see Prov. 31:10–31; 1 Peter 3:1–6)?

15. **4:2–6.** Read John 15:1–11. How do the means of grace (prayer, Bible reading, sitting under the preaching of God's word, the sacraments, and fellowship with God's people) help you to abide in Christ? In what areas do you need to grow in obedience to God's word and in absolute dependence on Jesus?

16. **5:1–30.** (a) How do you recognize, record, and recall for the next generation all that the Lord has done for you? If you're not in the habit of doing so, consider starting a prayer journal to help you.

(b) How has materialism tempted you and proven to be empty in fulfilling your deepest thirst? Which of the following have tempted you, failing to fulfill your needs: alcohol or another addiction, disbelief in God's presence and work, darkness (evil) in place of light (good), or self-righteousness?

(c) Meditate on John 4:13–14. How have you found Jesus's words to be true?

Putting It All Together...

Beauty beckoned me. Billboards and magazines surrounded me. Fine dresses and elegant scarves, sparkling rings and leather handbags, perfume and sophisticated hairstyles tempted me to define beauty by external appearance. Growing up in a materialistic culture tempted me to believe my worth was based on my appearance. Thankfully, the truth of Scripture taught me otherwise. I learned that the Lord looks at the heart, not at the outward appearance (1 Sam. 16:7). I learned that beauty is vain, but fearing the Lord is praiseworthy (Prov. 31:30). And I learned the value of storing up treasure in heaven instead of in this world (Matt. 6:19–21). Clearly, Scripture defines our worth differently from the way this world does. These chapters in Isaiah are one place that speaks forcefully about this issue. Bands, bracelets, boxes of perfume, bags, and belts don't buy us favor with the Lord. Our beauty before Him comes from the beauty of His Son, Jesus Christ, who robes us with His righteousness.

I. The Lord Contends (1:1–31)

The breadth and depth of Isaiah's message cannot be overemphasized. His ministry spanned the reigns of four kings of Judah: Uzziah (also known as Azariah, 767–740 BC); Jotham (750–735 BC); Ahaz (735–715 BC); and Hezekiah (715–686 BC). Isaiah's ministry began the year Uzziah died and weathered the stormy seas of the Assyrians attacking Israel, the Northern Kingdom, in 733 BC and taking them into exile. These introductory chapters present us with a summary of the entire book, and this first chapter introduces the summary.

With the cosmos as the courtroom, the covenant Lord calls His people to account for breaking the covenant. This was not just a king-servant relationship but also a father-son relationship. The Creator had been spurned by His creation. The covenant Lord had been forsaken by His covenant people. And the Father had been despised by the delight of His eyes. The people's problem was not isolated, as if shaping up in one area of their lives would remedy the rest. Their problem was full-orbed rebellion, from their head to their toes. They needed a makeover from the Maker of all the earth. And it wasn't just they who needed an overhaul but the land as well. The holy land that had been given to Israel by the Holy One who had chosen Israel was unholy through and through. For all practical purposes, it should have been destroyed like the immoral cities of Sodom and Gomorrah, but the covenant Lord is not a practical Lord. He is holy, and He purposed a remnant to survive to bring glory and honor to His great name.

The things that the covenant Lord had asked of His people—sacrifices, offerings, prayers, the observance of holy days—were the things He asked them to stop doing. Empty of meaning are those things done with hands but without heart. Evil and injustice cannot coexist with God's goodness and justice. Yet in this chapter is a glorious note of hope. Scarlet sins can turn to snow. Crimson curses can become beautiful blessings. The city of rebelliousness and faithlessness can become the city of righteousness and faithfulness. But the heart must move from refusal and rebellion to willingness and obedience. Redemption and repentance must occur, or we will not be saved. Those who forsake the Lord will face an eternity in hell, but those who fear Him will face an eternity in heaven.

This chapter begs an answer to the question, How will Zion be redeemed by justice, and how will penitents be redeemed by righteousness? Jesus Christ is both just and the justifier. The Holy One of Israel does not disregard sin but deals with it through the covenant of redemption, in which the Father has appointed His people's redemption, the Son accomplishes it on the cross of Calvary, and the Holy Spirit applies it. The Spirit awakens sinners to sin and brings them to true repentance so that they might inherit the eternal city of righteousness. All those who have been called and redeemed need to respond to such grace with gratitude. We must turn from our sinful ways to the Savior and strive to do good. We must pray for justice in our land and care for the needy. We must not go through the motions of religion apart from a growing relationship with Christ. And we must turn from our rebelliousness in our relationships and seek righteousness.

II. The Lord Consoles (2:1–4:6)

This section, which continues the theme of confrontation that we saw in chapter 1, is bracketed with two sections of consolation (2:2–4 and 4:2–6). These two notes of gracious hope sounded on the front end and back end of confrontation are intentional and give us a glimpse of the answer to the question, Have God's promises failed to Israel because of their rebellion? Isaiah answers with a resounding no. God's promise to Abraham to bless all the nations through him (Gen. 12:3) would be fulfilled in the latter days. The covenant Lord would establish a mountain on which worshipers would worship in spirit and in truth. Nations would flow to it, and they would want to walk in His ways.

The Prince of Peace would come, bringing light into the world. His death would create one new man out of the two, killing hostility. At His ascension, He would send the Spirit, and nations would understand the gospel in their own tongues. This gospel message is what we must console people with today when they are confronted with their sin. The depth of our sinfulness is great, to be sure, but the depth of God's grace is far greater.

It is precisely the depth of sinfulness that the covenant Lord confronts Judah with in between the messages of consolation (Isa. 2:5–4:1). They had not been a light to the nations but instead were captivated by the sight of the nations and what those nations had. The idolatry invigorated them. The treasures tantalized them. And the beauty beckoned them. But before they could reach the height of exaltation that they wanted to attain, the Lord reminded them that He alone is the exalted One of all the earth (2:17). He alone is judge. Yet Israel continued fearing man instead of the Holy One of Israel. So covenant curses would fall on their land. Jerusalem would fall because they failed to fear the faithful One and bear fruitful deeds.

Although Jerusalem would fall, the Lord promised that it would be well with the righteous (Isa. 3:10). The Branch of the Lord, the descendant of David, would be born in Bethlehem beautiful and glorious. His holiness would be credited to God's people. His blood would wash away the filth of their sins. God's people would come to Mount Zion, the city of the living God, in which the cross of Christ would shelter them from the terror of the Lord. Hidden in Him, we will not have to hide in holes in the ground but will bow before Him as we behold His beautiful face and cry out, "Holy!" It is His holiness that enables our holiness, His power that enables our practice. Let us strive then for holiness, without which no one will see the Lord (Heb. 12:14).

III. The Lord Condemns (5:1–30)

Striking in chapter 5 is the absence of a note of hope. As the curtain closes on the introduction to the book of Isaiah, we are left shrouded in darkness. It is the darkness you feel when a covenant promise, like marriage vows, has been broken. This chapter begins with a lover's broken heart. The covenant Lord had chosen Israel to be His bride. He had gone above and beyond His call of duty as a husband. He had loved her and led her well with His words and works. But she would have none of it. Instead, she exchanged righteousness for unrighteousness and justice for injustice. Therefore, the Lord condemned her.

Israel and Judah were without excuse. They exchanged God for greed. They exchanged their Maker for materialism. They exchanged the Almighty for alcohol. They exchanged praise of the personal God for parties. They exchanged reverence for rudeness. They exchanged sweet for sour. They exchanged wisdom for worth in their own eyes. And they exchanged justice for judgment. Therefore, the Holy One of Israel became angry. He would use the nations they had had an affair with to attack them and put them in exile.

Robert Murray McCheyne (1813–1843), a Scottish pastor, said, "For every look at yourself, take ten looks at Christ."[1] Let this then be the one look at yourself in this chapter. This is an apt description of all of us. We are adulterers and idolaters at heart. We exchange our Creator for the creation time and again. Every part of us is corrupted with sin. Though we try, we cannot be good. Our hearts, heads, and hands are filled with darkness. This chapter should result in a cry for a deliverer. Apart from the Savior, we all stand condemned before the Holy God, Maker of heaven and earth.

When has beauty according to this world beckoned you? These chapters remind us that beauty comes from Christ. United to Him, we strive to be holy as our heavenly Father is holy. We turn from the adultery and idolatry of this world to the awesome and immortal God who knows us by name, calls us by His grace, and sustains us by His grace to live a life that glorifies Him.

---

1. Robert Murray McCheyne, *Memoir and Remains of the Rev. Robert Murray McCheyne* (Edinburgh, 1894), 293.

Processing It Together...

1. What do we learn about God in Isaiah 1–5?

2. How does this reshape how we should view our present circumstances?

3. What do we learn about God's Son, Jesus Christ?

4. How should this impact our relationship with God and with others?

5. What do we learn about God's covenant with His people?

6. How are we to live in light of this?

7. How can we apply Isaiah 1–5 to our lives today and in the future?

8. How should we apply this passage in our churches?

9. Look back at "Put It in Perspective" in your personal study questions. What did you find challenging or encouraging about this lesson?

10. Look back at "Principles and Points of Application." How has this lesson impacted your life?

The Holy Lord Sends

Isaiah 6–12

Purpose...

Head. What do I need to know from this passage in Scripture?

- The holy Lord sends Isaiah, invaders, and Immanuel to His people.

Heart. How does what I learn from this passage affect my internal relationship with the Lord?

- I am a kingdom disciple who has been saved from my sins by my Savior, Jesus Christ, so that I can sing of His salvation and trust in Him all my days.

Hands. How does what I learn from this passage translate into action for God's kingdom?

- I will teach others of God's holiness, our sinfulness, and the good news of the Savior.

- I will pray for the Lord to save my unbelieving family members and friends.

- I will pray for the salvation of the nations and participate in the Great Commission by going, sending, or both.

- I will lead those under my care to praise the Lord for who He is and what He has done.

Personal Study...

Pray. Ask that God will open up your heart and mind as you study His Word. This is His story of redemption that He has revealed to us, and the Holy Spirit is our teacher.

Ponder the Passage. Read Isaiah 6–12.

- *Point.* What is the point of this passage? How does this relate to the point of the entire book?

- *Persons.* Who are the main people involved in this passage? What characterizes them?

- *Persons of the Trinity.* Where do you see God the Father, God the Son, and God the Holy Spirit in this passage?

- *Puzzling Parts.* Are there any parts of the passage that you don't quite understand or that seem interesting or confusing?

Put It in Perspective.

- *Place in Scripture.* What is the original context of this text? What is the redemptive-historical context—what has or hasn't happened in redemptive history at this point in Scripture? How does this text connect to Christ?

The following questions will help you if you got stuck on any of the previous questions, and they will help you dig a little deeper into the text, putting it all into perspective.

1. **6:1–8.** (a) What kind of king was Uzziah (see 2 Chronicles 26)? How is the King of kings far greater?

(b) Which of God's attributes comes to the forefront in these verses? How does Isaiah show it?

(c) What does it mean that God is holy?

(d) How far does the Lord's glory extend?

(e) What do you learn about the sinfulness of man in light of the holiness of God?

(f) What do you learn about the solution for sin in these verses?

(g) How is atonement ultimately made for sin (see Heb. 10:11–14)?

2. **6:9–13.** (a) What kind of response can Isaiah expect from both Israel (the Northern Kingdom) and Judah (the Southern Kingdom)? How did this prove true in Jesus's day as well as Paul's (see Matt. 13:10–17; John 12:37–43; Acts 28:23–28)?

(b) How are both the judgment of exile and the promise of restoration seen in these verses?

(c) Who is the holy seed (see Gen. 3:15; Luke 1:31–35)?

3. **7:1–17.** (a) Who should Ahaz have feared instead of Israel and Syria, and why?

(b) What mistake did he make in his fear (see 2 Kings 16:5–9)?

(c) How is verse 9 a summary statement of all Isaiah's exhortations you've read so far in this book?

(d) How is Isaiah's son's name, Shear-Jashub ("a remnant shall return"), encouraging?

(e) What sign did the Lord give to self-righteous Ahaz? To whom does the sign ultimately point (see Matt. 1:18–23)?

(f) Who will be the Lord's instrument of judgment on Israel?

4. **7:18–8:8.** (a) How are these verses an apt description of the covenant curses that will fall on Israel (see Lev. 26:14–22)?

(b) On whom do the covenant curses for God's people ultimately fall (see Matt. 26:26–29; 27:32–54)?

(c) How is the name of Isaiah's son, Maher-Shalal-Hash-Baz, a word of judgment against Israel (see 2 Kings 15:29)?

(d) By rejecting the waters of Shiloah, whom did they ultimately reject (see John 9:11)?

(e) What impact will the Assyrian king have on Judah?

5. **8:9–22.** (a) What is the remnant's hope and security?

(b) How does Peter use verse 12 in the context of his letter (see 1 Peter 3:14–15)?

(c) What are Paul and Peter saying when they quote verse 14 (see Rom. 9:33; 1 Peter 2:8)?

(d) What is the author of Hebrews saying when he uses verse 18 (see Heb. 2:13)?

(e) What had the Lord instructed His people regarding the occult, and why (see Lev. 19:31; Deut. 18:9–14)?

6. **9:1–7.** (a) How does the phrase "Galilee of the Gentiles" point back to God's promise to Abraham in Genesis 12:3? How is this ultimately fulfilled (see Matt. 4:13–17; Eph. 2:14–18)?

(b) How do these verses continue to describe the Immanuel promised in 7:14?

(c) Using your cross references, list and look up New Testament verses that demonstrate Christ has fulfilled these verses.

7. **9:8–10:4.** (a) What phrase do you find repeatedly in these verses?

(b) Why is the Lord just in His judgment (see Deut. 28:15–68)?

8. **10:5–15.** (a) How was the king of Assyria deceived by his arrogant heart?

(b) How is this a reflection of all humankind (see Jer. 17:9–10)?

(c) How do these verses reveal the need for Christ?

9. 10:16–34. (a) What do you learn about the remnant of Israel in these verses?

(b) How will the Lord deal with the king of Assyria, and why?

(c) How does the remnant reveal God's faithfulness to His promises and anticipate the Messiah?

(d) What is Paul saying in Romans 9:14–28, and why does he use Isaiah 10:22 in this context?

10. 11:1–16. (a) What do you learn about God the Son and God the Holy Spirit in verses 1–5?

(b) How do these verses anticipate the inauguration and consummation of Christ's kingdom (Luke 1:31–33; Rev. 19:11–16)?

(c) How do these verses anticipate the fulfillment of God's promise in Genesis 12:3 (see also Rev. 21:24, 26)?

(d) What is Paul saying in Romans 15:7–12, and why does he use Isaiah 11:10 in this context?

(e) How is verse 12 ultimately fulfilled in Matthew 24:31?

11. 12:1–6. (a) Why would these words have comforted God's people? How were they to respond to God's gracious salvation?

(b) How do these verses look back toward the great act of salvation in Exodus 14–15 and forward to the great salvation recorded in the Gospels?

Principles and Points of Application

12. 6:1–13. (a) How does the Lord's kingship over the entire world and His holiness help you understand your utter sinfulness before Him and your desperate need for God's grace? How are you teaching these truths to those under your care?

(b) Think about someone you know who is hardened to the gospel. Why do these verses remind you to continue crying out to God, the only Savior, for their salvation? Spend time in prayer for them.

13. 7:1–17. (a) In what situation are you tempted to fear man instead of having quiet confidence in the Lord your God? Confess this to Him, and ask Him to fill you with trust in Him.

(b) How could you use 7:9b to share the gospel with your friend or to help your child cope with anxiety and fear?

(c) Why does the name Immanuel comfort you (see Matt. 1:23)? How could you use it to comfort someone you know? Plan to do that.

14. 7:18–8:8. (a) How do these verses remind you to find your solace in the Lord and Savior, Jesus Christ, who has taken the covenant curses on Himself?

(b) Have you received Jesus Christ as Lord and Savior of your life, or have you refused His living water of eternal life that He freely offers?

15. 8:9–22. (a) How are you tempted to walk in the way of the world instead of honoring the Lord as holy, fearing Him, and hoping in Him?

(b) Is there something in your future about which you wish you knew the outcome? How do these verses encourage you to hope in God?

(c) How could you use these verses to encourage a friend not to trust in horoscopes and other occult arts but to trust in Christ?

16. 9:1–7. Read through these verses, inserting the name Jesus Christ each time it's appropriate. What one name or description of Christ encourages you the most, and why?

17. 9:8–10:4. It's only because of Christ, the covenant keeper, that God's anger turns away from believers. Otherwise, it is still outstretched against all those in rebellion against Him. Spend time in prayer for unbelievers you know, asking the Lord to turn away His anger from them by saving their souls.

18. 10:5–15. Examine your heart, asking the Lord to expose any arrogance you have in your attitude and actions.

19. **10:16–34.** In what ways are you leaning on someone or something other than the Lord instead of on the Lord, the Holy One, in truth?

20. **11:1–16.** Why do these verses encourage you to pray for the salvation of the nations and to participate in the Great Commission by going, sending, or both?

21. **12:1–6.** (a) Write out these verses, personalizing them for your specific circumstances.

(b) How are you leading those under your care to constant praise and thanksgiving for who the Lord is and what He has done?

Putting It All Together...

I can distinctly recall different times in my life when I was so overwhelmed with my sin that I was brought to my knees in repentance and tears. During these times I was keenly aware that I could not stand before the Holy God. I recognized my desperate need for the Lord and Savior Jesus Christ to be my Great High Priest. I felt small and weak before the King of all the earth. And I was aware that I had failed to obey His word. These times left me very shaken. Yet afterward I had a renewed sense of gratitude for the redemptive work God the Father has appointed, Jesus Christ has accomplished, and the Holy Spirit has applied. I was able to sing of God's comfort and grace as I once again recognized that He is my salvation.

A profound sense of our sinfulness and God's gracious forgiveness should always result in worship, which becomes our greatest witness to the world around us. In chapters 6–12 Isaiah comes face-to-face with the kingship and holiness of God, with his sinfulness, and with the hope of forgiveness. Such a profound experience led the prophet to go where God sent him, firm in his faith and singing of God's salvation. May these chapters do the same for us.

I. The Holy Lord Sends Isaiah (6:1–7:17)

With chapters 1–5, the introduction to the book of Isaiah, still echoing in our minds, we now learn of several prominent themes that will take center stage in Isaiah's message. First, there is no one so great, so glorious, and so holy as the King of kings, the Lord God, the Holy One of the entire earth. No king in Israel could begin to compare with His holiness and righteousness, His otherness. Second, the holiness of God is what sets Him apart as completely other. God's holiness is not just a characteristic of His being but a comprehensive summary of who God is. Third, His dominion is not limited in any way to just one nation or nations; it is over the entire world. Fourth, all humankind is lost in darkness and stands before the Holy God as unclean. Every person is a sinner in need of atonement from the Savior. Finally, this Savior, this holy Seed, will atone for the sins of God's people. Isaiah, chosen to be a servant of God to take the message of both judgment and hope to God's people, first learned the lesson they would soon learn. The holy King cannot tolerate the sinfulness of His people. But instead of failing to fulfill His promises, the Holy God raises up the solution to sin in the promised Savior.

Isaiah's first speaking engagement was with King Ahaz, who reigned over Judah from 732/31–716/15 BC. When Ahaz learned that the king of Israel had made an alliance with the king of Syria in order to attack his land, Jerusalem, he was very scared. In his fear, he made a grave mistake. He reached out to the king of Assyria for help (2 Kings 16:5–9). The Lord sent Isaiah and his son to Ahaz with a hard message. Even so, the meaning of Isaiah's son's name, "a remnant shall return," spoke of God's faithfulness and gave a word of hope. In the face of Syria and Israel's fierce anger, Ahaz was not to fear or be fainthearted and was to quietly, confidently, and carefully stand firm in faith that God's word regarding Israel and Syria's destruction was true. The Lord even invited Ahaz to ask of Him a sign, but Ahaz's self-reliance prevailed and he refused (Isa. 7:10–11). So the Lord gave him a sign. A virgin would conceive and bear a son who would be named Immanuel, "God with us" (v. 14). He would refuse evil and choose good. This sign was given as a token and a pledge that the king of Assyria would shatter both Israel and Syria.

How hard it is for us to stand firm in faith in the face of fear! We know the temptation Ahaz faced all too well. The phone call comes from the doctor's office that something threatens our health. The history on our husband's computer shows that pornography is a problem for him. The bitter words spoken by a person we thought was a friend wound us. Our child walks out the door of our home and away from the faith we hold so dear. The progress of our child who has a developmental delay is painfully slow, and we wonder if he'll ever catch up to his peers. This section in Isaiah reminds us to quiet our hearts, be careful of whom and what we fear, and keep firm in the faith. Our great King is holy and has dominion over the whole world. Who or what should we fear when He is on our side? In Christ we are more than conquerors. He quiets us by His loving faithfulness and remains the sign of all signs that God is with us.

II. The Holy Lord Sends Invaders (7:18–8:22)

Like bees that swarm from a hive, the Lord would send the Assyrians into the land He had given to Israel (Isa. 7:18–19). The promised land of blessing would be filled with the briers and thorns of judgment (v. 24). The judgment on Adam is revisited on Israel and will be revisited on the true Israel, the Suffering Servant, Jesus Christ. Isaiah's first son had a name filled with promise. His second son's name means "the spoil speeds, the prey hastens"—a name filled with judgment, which spelled doom for Syria and Israel at the hand of the Assyrians (8:3–4).

How different it could have been! If only God's people hadn't refused Him, the One who makes the waters of Shiloah flow gently (Isa. 8:6). But instead they had rejoiced over Syria and Israel, and so the Lord would bring the king of Assyria to the brink of Jerusalem. Like a looming shadow covering the chosen city, threatening destruction, the king of Assyria would draw near to Immanuel's land.

Jesus declared to His disciples that He was the light of the world and then followed His declaration with a miraculous healing of a blind man using the waters of Siloam (John 9:5–7). Jesus's light- and sight-giving water are offered to all who will turn from the fear of man and the saviors of this world to Him. As long as we trust in human-kind, dark shadows of judgment loom over us. Our safety is only in the shadow of the Almighty's wings. Christ has come to set us free from the prey that hastens so that we can have peace in Him.

Not everyone in Israel had forsaken the Lord. He always preserves a remnant to worship Him. So it was in Isaiah's day. Their hope and security was the Lord of hosts, the one they honored as holy. Yet it was difficult to be faithful in the midst of a rebel-lious people. So the Lord provided a strong exhortation to Isaiah and the remnant, as well as a warning for those who didn't fear Him. He was a sanctuary for the remnant but a stone of stumbling for the rebellious Israelites.

Instead of walking in the way of the rebellious, the Lord's disciples were to keep the word of the Lord central (Isa. 8:16). Their hope was to be in Him. The remnant became a sign and wonder in Israel, testifying of His grace. Instead of following the ways of the land and seeking mediums and wizards, as the majority of Israel had done, the remnant was to seek the light through God's word. Those who sought the dark-ness would see darkness and be driven into it (v. 22). The Lord had warned His people about this darkness: "Give no regard to mediums and familiar spirits; do not seek after them, to be defiled by them: I am the LORD your God" (Lev. 19:31; see also Deut. 18:9–14). In contrast, those who seek light will see light and be delivered by it. Jesus is the light of the world (John 8:12). His disciples are to seek Him.

Peter picks up Isaiah 8:12 in writing about suffering for righteousness' sake (1 Peter 3:14–15). Like the remnant in Isaiah's day, the righteous sufferer is blessed and need not be afraid or troubled by the unrighteous. Instead, the righteous are to sanctify the Lord in their hearts and be ready to defend the hope that is within them with meek-ness and fear. Peter also uses Isaiah 8:14 in explaining the difference Christ makes in the life of the believer and the unbeliever. For the believer, Christ is precious. For the unbeliever, Christ is a stone of stumbling (1 Peter 2:8). Paul also quotes from Isaiah 8:14, stating that Israel stumbled at that stumbling stone (Rom. 9:32–33). In addition, the author of Hebrews quotes from Isaiah 8 when he mentions Christ unashamedly calling Christians His brethren. Christ is the elder brother leading God's people in worship, presenting Himself and the children God has given Him, in an act of praise and worship (Heb. 2:11–13; see Isa. 8:18).

Do you see what's happening here? In the midst of very bad news in Isaiah's day, there was very good news. The Lord had preserved a remnant, and in the midst of darkness, they had light in Him. In the midst of chaos, they had a sanctuary in Him. As Peter, Paul, and the author of Hebrews make clear, the same is true during this time of redemptive history. Judgment is coming, but the Lord's people are safe in Him. Let us not lose heart in suffering for doing good. Christ has brought us to God! The Singer of singers leads us in praise, comforts us in suffering, and is our light in the darkness.

III. The Holy Lord Sends Immanuel (9–12)

Rays of hope fill these chapters. Immanuel is not just a sign. Immanuel is a person who will come, bringing salvation to the nations (Isa. 9:1–7). Gloom, anguish, and contempt will give way to glory as the Light of the world shines on God's people. The Christ child will rule the nations. He is not just a descendant of David; He is the one from whom Jesse and David's line originated. He is the King of kings who will rule in perfect righteousness and justice. It is because He is just, holy, and righteous that His anger cannot turn away, and His hand remains outstretched on covenant breakers (9:8–10:4). The holy Lord cannot overlook sin. He must deal with it. Though He uses Assyria as an instrument of judgment in His hand, His anger will not turn away from the proud Assyrians. Ultimately, He will bring them to utter ruin (10:5–19).

But because Immanuel is both just and justifier, there can be a remnant, and indeed there will be a remnant that will return under the hand of the mighty God (Isa. 10:20–34; 11:10–16). He will save a remnant from every tribe, tongue, and nation to dwell with Him forever in the new heavens and the new earth and to sing praises and give thanks to Him, the Lamb that was slain to atone for the sins of God's people (12:1–6). It is only in Christ that God's anger is turned away from us. Jesus has kept the covenant for us so that we might be saved. There is comfort for us in Christ—our salvation, strength, and song. When the Lord led Israel out of Egypt, Moses and the people of Israel sang a song exalting the Lord's victory (Ex. 15:1–21). Today we sing of a greater exodus. Christ has delivered God's people from sin and death through the cross. We can sing praises to Him because He has first sung a song of salvation over us. We can comfort others because He has first comforted us. Let us make known His deeds among all peoples, praying for salvation to come to the nations.

It's likely that you can relate to me and the times I came face-to-face with my sin and my desperate need of God's salvation. Such times should leave us singing a song of praise and thanksgiving to our great and Holy God. We can trust in Him when the storms of life threaten to undo us. The water from the wells of salvation will never run dry. Our call on His name will never go unheard. He is glorious and has done glorious things. Now we have the privilege and the responsibility to proclaim His word and His works to those around us. Let us be faithful to do so, firm in the faith, with eyes on the thrice-holy King.

Processing It Together...

1. What do we learn about God in Isaiah 6–12?

2. How does this reshape how we should view our present circumstances?

3. What do we learn about God's Son, Jesus Christ?

4. How should this impact our relationship with God and with others?

5. What do we learn about God's covenant with His people?

6. How are we to live in light of this?

7. How can we apply Isaiah 6–12 to our lives today and in the future?

8. How should we apply this passage in our churches?

9. Look back at "Put It in Perspective" in your personal study questions. What did you find challenging or encouraging about this lesson?

10. Look back at "Principles and Points of Application." How has this lesson impacted your life?

The Lord of Hosts Reigns

Isaiah 13–27

Purpose...

Head. What do I need to know from this passage in Scripture?

- The Lord of hosts reigns over the nations and the entire earth with a rod of iron, which is ultimately fulfilled in King Jesus, who receives the nations as His heritage and the earth as His possession.

Heart. How does what I learn from this passage affect my internal relationship with the Lord?

- I am a kingdom disciple who is united to Christ, the ruler of the nations. Therefore, I can exalt Him in my heart, praising His holy name, rejoicing in His salvation, and living in peace as I trust in Him.

Hands. How does what I learn from this passage translate into action for God's kingdom?

- I will take part in making disciples of all nations, knowing that the Lord is building His church, which is made up of people from every tribe, tongue, and nation.
- I will help others stop seeking the honors of this world and look to Christ, the highly honored One.
- I will encourage those around me to live in eager expectation of eternity with the triune God.

Personal Study...

Pray. Ask that God will open up your heart and mind as you study His Word. This is His story of redemption that He has revealed to us, and the Holy Spirit is our teacher.

Ponder the Passage. Read Isaiah 13–27. Since there are fifteen chapters to read this week, I recommend studying and answering questions on three chapters a day. For example, on day 1 read and answer only questions for Isaiah 13–15.

- *Point.* What is the point of this passage? How does this relate to the point of the entire book?

- *Persons.* Who are the main people involved in this passage? What characterizes them?

- *Persons of the Trinity.* Where do you see God the Father, God the Son, and God the Holy Spirit in this passage?

- *Puzzling Parts.* Are there any parts of the passage that you don't quite understand or that seem interesting or confusing?

Put It in Perspective.

- *Place in Scripture.* What is the original context of this text? What is the redemptive-historical context—what has or hasn't happened in redemptive history at this point in Scripture? How does this text connect to Christ?

The following questions will help you if you got stuck on any previous questions, and they will help you dig a little deeper into the text, putting it all into perspective.

1. **13:1–14:27.** (a) Beginning with Genesis 11 and ending with Revelation 18, what does Babel/Babylon symbolize in Scripture?

   (b) How does the day of the Lord (13:6, 9) mentioned here relate to the final day of the Lord in Revelation 19:11–20:15?

   (c) How do we see the Lord's absolute sovereignty in these verses?

(d) How do we see the Lord's compassion on His people?

(e) How are the arrogance and iniquity we read about in these chapters related to Genesis 3?

(f) What is the end of every Sodom and Gomorrah, as well as Babylon and Assyria, and why?

2. **14:28–32.** (a) Why was Philistia not a good place for God's people to turn for security after King Ahaz died? Where was the nation to turn?

(b) What does verse 32 have to do with Hebrews 12:22–24?

3. **15:1–16:14.** (a) What were Moab's vices?

(b) What do these verses reveal about the glory of man in light of the glory of the Lord?

(c) Who reveals the glory of the Lord (see John 1:14)?

4. **17:1–18:7.** (a) According to 17:3, what happens to Ephraim (Israel), and why (see 2 Kings 16:1–9; Isa. 7:3–9; 17:10)?

(b) According to 17:7–8, what is the solution to sin?

(c) How does the New Testament answer the previous question (see, for example, Heb. 9:11–15; 12:1–2), and how does 18:7 anticipate Revelation 21:24–26?

5. **19:1–20:6.** (a) Why shouldn't God's people put their trust in Egypt?

(b) To whom will some in Egypt ultimately turn (19:19–22)?

(c) How are Egypt, Assyria, and Israel connected? How does this fulfill God's promise in Genesis 12:3 and anticipate Acts 2:5–13; 11:18; Revelation 7:4, 9?

(d) How did Isaiah suffer for his faith? How does his suffering anticipate Matthew 5:10–11; James 1:2–4; 1 Peter 1:6–9?

6. **21:1–10.** (a) Where have we already seen an oracle regarding Babylon? How does Isaiah respond to the Lord's words?

(b) How does this oracle, like the one in 13:1–14:27, look back at Genesis 11:1–9 and forward to Revelation 18? What does verse 9 have in common with Revelation 14:8 and 18:2? How do these verses relate?

7. **21:11–17.** (a) How is the glory of man swallowed by the glory of the Lord?

(b) How do you see the power of God's spoken word in these verses?

8. 22:1–25. (a) Why is Isaiah speaking of the future as if it's already accomplished in verses 3–7?

(b) For background on verses 8–11, see 2 Kings 20:20; 2 Chronicles 32:2–4.

(c) What is Israel's primary sin? How does Paul use verse 13 in 1 Corinthians 15:32?

(d) How do Shebna and Eliakim reveal different ways humankind seeks security?

(e) Who is the only person who can secure the kingdom of God (see Rev. 3:7)? Who later wept, like Isaiah, over Jerusalem (see Matt. 23:1, 37–39)?

9. 23:1–18. (a) Why shouldn't God's people trust in Tyre or in everything Tyre symbolized?

(b) How do verses 17–18 anticipate Revelation 17:1–2 and 21:24–26?

10. 24:1–23. (a) How does this chapter recall both the fall in Genesis 3 and the flood in Genesis 6–9, especially 7:11 and 9:16, 20, 25?

(b) In the midst of judgment upon the rebellious, what are God's people doing (vv. 13–16a)?

(c) How do these verses anticipate Revelation 4:11; 5:9–10; 11:17–18; 15:3–4; 19:1–8?

11. 25:1–12. (a) How does the Lord reveal He is the Savior?

(b) How do verses 6–8 reflect Exodus 24:9–11?

(c) How does Paul use verse 8 in 1 Corinthians 15:54?

(d) What do you learn about joy in John 15:9–11?

12. 26:1–21. (a) How do these verses specifically reveal the Lord's zeal for His people, as well as His glorious justice on the wicked?

(b) What New Testament teaching does verse 19 anticipate?

(c) How do verses 20–21 reflect Genesis 7:1, 16 and Exodus 12:22–23?

13. 27:1–13. (a) How does the chapter declare God's triumph over evil and His faithfulness to His covenant promises to His people?

(b) How do verses 12–13 anticipate Matthew 24:31; 1 Corinthians 15:52; and 1 Thessalonians 4:16?

Principles and Points of Application
14. 13:1–20:6. (a) How are these chapters on God's judgment of the nations and on the pride of the ruthless rulers of this world an encouragement to you? What do they have to say about God's purposes and His compassion that encourage you?

(b) In what ways are you afflicted today? How are you finding refuge in Christ?

(c) Examine your heart for arrogance and idle boasting. Spend time in confession and repentance before the Lord, who invites you to come before the throne of grace.

(d) In what area(s) of your life are you tempted to forget the God of your salvation and the rock of your refuge? Turn away from introspection and idolatry and look to your Maker, the Holy One of Israel. Spend time worshiping Him and casting your cares at His feet.

(e) Since you know that the Lord is building His church, made up of people from every tribe, tongue, and nation, how are you taking part in making disciples of all nations?

15. **21:1–23:18.** (a) How does Isaiah's response to the Lord's judgment challenge you or convict you as you think about your response to Scripture's teaching about the final day of the Lord?

(b) In what ways are you seeking glory for yourself? How do these chapters convict you to live for God's glory alone?

(c) How do you try to secure your own achievements (for example, by finances, beauty, or some other worldly thing) instead of looking to the Lord? Or in what way are you putting your trust in another person for security instead of in the Lord God?

(d) How are you challenged in these chapters to stop seeking the honors of this world and look to Christ, the highly honored One?

16. 24:1–27:13. (a) What darkness is threatening you (for example, a health, financial, or marriage crisis)? How does 24:14–16a encourage you?

(b) Write out a song of joy to the Lord. Memorize 26:3–4.

(c) How are you taking part in the Lord enlarging the borders of His church and kingdom?

(d) How does your eager expectation of Christ's second coming and eternity with Him affect the way you live your life?

Putting It All Together...

It is incredibly difficult, in the hour of greatest need, not to turn to the things of this world for security. When our health is at its worst, when our teenager confesses she's been binging and purging, when our adult child professes to be gay, when our bank account dwindles to almost nothing, when our employer says he's cutting our job, and when our aging parents require more of our time and care, we want to cling to medicine, treatment plans, the lottery, or some other worldly thing to bring security and stability to our lives. But Scripture shows repeatedly that this is the wrong move to make. Of course, medicine and treatment plans may be good and necessary for certain situations, but they cannot be our confidence. Our confidence must be in Christ.

In these chapters of Isaiah we learn that in the hour of darkest need, God's people were tempted to turn to surrounding nations for security. By showing the judgment coming to the nations by the hand of the almighty God, Isaiah aims to convince them that such security is false. It's a poignant reminder for you and me as we are tempted to secure our present and future in the things or relationships of this world. Only in Christ will perfect peace be found.

I. The Lord of Hosts Musters a Host for Battle (13–20)

The previous chapter closed with Israel's mission statement—to declare the deeds of the Holy One of Israel among the surrounding nations so that God's name would be exalted (Isa. 12:4–6). In this lesson we will learn that Israel failed to carry out their mission, and consequently the surrounding nations, as well as Israel, were judged because of their pride, disbelief, and rebellion. Yet at the same time, Israel takes center stage in these oracles about the nations, reminding us that even though Israel failed, the Lord's purposes will not be thwarted. Not only will salvation come to Israel but to nations like Egypt and Assyria as well.

The first oracle in this cycle concerns Babylon (Isa. 13:1–22) and Assyria (14:24–27), and not just Babylon the nation but everything that Babylon had come to symbolize in redemptive history, beginning with the Tower of Babel in Genesis 11. Babylon is code for "me-ism" (life is all about my position, power, and prestige). In the historical context, with Assyria as the world's superpower, Israel was tempted to tether its anchor to a nation like Babylon. But Isaiah reveals Babylon for what it really is—a nation ripe for judgment because of its pompous pride. Its splendor conceals its need for salvation, and its rebellion covers its need for redemption. Babylon delights in bringing pain, turmoil, and hard service to God's people, but in the end the Lord will cut off its name that it made for itself and bring it to utter destruction.

Notes of grace interrupt an otherwise difficult oracle filled with judgment (Isa. 14:1–23). The Lord of hosts is sovereignly bringing to pass His purposes for His people. He will have compassion on them. The Lord will also give His people rest. And He will break the staff of the wicked. In the second oracle in this cycle against Philistia (vv. 28–32), we learn that the city of Zion that He founded will remain a refuge for His people (v. 32).

The third oracle in this cycle concerns Moab (Isa. 15:1–16:14), and again Isaiah is arguing that God's people should not turn to them for help. No one except the Holy One of Israel can save them. But they are constantly tempted to reach out to the nations around them for salvation. Moab is not a good choice for the same reasons Babylon isn't a good choice. He is proud, insolent, and boastful (16:6). Yet again there's a note of grace embedded in this oracle. A Davidic throne will be established in steadfast love, and the king will reign in justice and righteousness (v. 5).

The fourth oracle concerns Israel and Damascus (Isa. 17:1–18:7). Israel had wrongly sought an alliance with Syria (see Isa. 7:1–16; 8:1–4) during Isaiah's day, and the prophet reproves them by revealing Damascus's end. Why would Israel put their trust in Damascus when it would become a heap of ruins? Forgetting their Savior and rock of refuge was costly for Israel. Yet again, there's a note of hope. The Lord will preserve a remnant that will look to their Maker instead of to their makings (17:7–8).

God's judgment against Cush highlights an interesting dimension (Isa. 18:1–7). There are times when the Lord quietly looks from His dwelling on the evil going on in His world instead of acting swiftly. Yet for all the talk of judgment, there's again a note of grace in this oracle. When the Lord returns at the end of history to usher in the new heavens and the new earth, tribute will be brought to heavenly Zion from the Gentile nations (Isa. 18:7; Rev. 21:24–26).

The fifth oracle in this cycle concerns Egypt (Isa. 19:1–20:6). The Nile was no match for the Name above all names. The Egyptians' wisdom became useless before the wise

One of all the earth. The Lord brought confusion where they boasted in clarity. Yet even here judgment is not the final word. The Lord of hosts will raise up a remnant from both Egypt and Assyria. Israel should learn a lesson. If even Egypt and Assyria will ultimately turn to the Lord for salvation, why isn't Israel turning to Him now? If the covenant Lord will claim Egypt and Assyria alongside Israel as His covenant people, why would Israel turn to them for deliverance instead of to Yahweh? At the Lord's command, Isaiah went so far as to walk around naked and barefoot for three years to give Israel a picture of what would happen to Egypt and Cush as they were taken into exile by Assyria (20:2). Does Israel really want to trust in nations that would one day be naked in shame?

Behind the darkness of each of these five oracles shines the bright light of the gospel. The Lord of hosts is over all battles in the history of the world. It is certain that good will triumph over evil. The Lord will have compassion on His chosen people, and this people will come from every tribe, tongue, and nation. Rest will come through the righteous Davidic king who will reign from Zion. The Lord's purposes will not be thwarted by human pride. The God of salvation and rock of refuge will raise the multitude's eyes to their Maker in praise. Both Jews and Gentiles will flow to the heavenly Zion to worship King Jesus, the final Davidic king, who reigns in justice and righteousness. Because of Christ, the Lord will listen to our pleas for mercy and heal us. In Christ we are His people, the work of His hands, and His inheritance.

With such amazing grace shining forth through the darkness, these chapters call for a response from us. Will we trust in the altars of this world, such as materialism, and the work of our hands, such as our achievements, or will we turn to the God of our salvation, the rock of our refuge, and trust in Him? His ears are open to hear your pleas for mercy, and His nail-pierced hands are outstretched to heal you. If you have never put your trust in Christ as your Lord and Savior, today is the day of salvation.

II. The Lord of Hosts Has Purposed His Own Glory (21–23)

This second cycle of five oracles, like the first, begins with Babylon (Isa. 21:1–10). But here again we learn that Isaiah isn't just denouncing the cities but also the sins the cities have come to symbolize. We must remember that the nations were not the ones hearing Isaiah's message; Israel was. Isaiah waved the red flag of warning, trying to convince God's people that those in whom they were tempted to put their trust were not trustworthy. Does a wilderness by the sea sound like a good place to go when one is in trouble? No, Babylon was doomed to fall because of its idolatry.

The second oracle concerns Edom (Isa. 21:11–12) and is a reminder that though God may be silent for a time, His sovereignty over the nations is still sure. God's people must be ready at all times for the Lord God to act.

The third oracle concerns Arabia (Isa. 21:13–17). Man's glory cannot stand before God's glory. The Lord God of Israel will not share His glory with another.

The fourth oracle concerns Jerusalem (Isa. 22:1–25). If only Israel would have had spiritual eyes in Jerusalem ("the valley of vision") to look to the Lord who accomplished and planned the city. Although Isaiah doesn't explain why he calls Jerusalem the valley of vision, it probably points to his distress as he thought about the unavoidable judgment of Jerusalem that God had revealed to him (v. 14).[1] The people could not make atonement for such sin. It was too great against the Holy God. Neither could they try to save themselves like Shebna, "the king's right hand man," who trusted in his own strength and power instead of in God's, or put their trust in a man like Eliakim, "a reliable office holder," who seemed secure at first but would fall.[2] Isaiah's mention of the key of the house of David in this oracle sounds a note of hope. Ultimately King Jesus would sit on the throne and make it again a throne of honor to His Father's house. It is Christ who secures God's people through His life, death, resurrection, and ascension. We must respond by refusing to trust in ourselves or in any other person or thing. Instead, we must look to Jesus alone for our salvation.

The fifth and final oracle concerns Tyre (Isa. 23:1–14). Tyre's merchants were princes, their traders the honored of the earth. But Tyre became filled with pride, so the Lord purposed their downfall. Why would Israel put their trust in a stronghold that was destined for waste? In fact, Tyre's merchandise and wages would become holy to Israel's God. If Israel would only trust in the Lord, they would ultimately receive the fine things of Tyre.

This second cycle of five oracles is deeply convicting. How often do we trust in our position or possessions or in our family name? The Lord of hosts has purposed to display His glory in this world by exposing our idols. Whether He is silent for a time or swift to destruction, He will not give His glory to another. When will we stop prostituting ourselves with all the kingdoms of this world? The Lord of hosts warns us against such adultery and idolatry. If only we would turn to Him, the one who has atoned for our sins through the cross of Calvary, we would find deliverance.

III. The Lord of Hosts Reigns (24–27)

In the past two cycles of oracles, we have learned that the Lord of hosts reigns over particular nations, as well as over Israel. These chapters bring us to a crescendo—the Lord of hosts reigns over the entire world. As in the days of Noah, when wickedness had become so great that the Lord God sent a flood to destroy the inhabitants of the earth, except for Noah and his family, so here we see the Lord in judgment empties the earth (Isa. 24:1–3). Even the highest people of the earth will be brought under judgment (v. 4). Position and prestige can't save us. The curse that we first learned about in Genesis 3 devours the entirety of the earth. All those who raised their fists in rebellion against the Creator will be punished on the final day of the Lord. Yet in the midst of the day of judgment, we will also hear the most beautiful song of joy by

---

1. Motyer, *Prophecy of Isaiah*, 182.
2. Motyer, *Prophecy of Isaiah*, 186.

the redeemed (vv. 14–16a). They will sing of the Lord's majesty and glory, exalting His name and righteousness. The Lord of hosts reigns, and the kingdoms of this world will consummately become the kingdom of His Son.

Those whom the Lord of hosts saves will exalt and praise His name, recognizing the wondrous things He has done and His faithfulness. The poor and needy will at last have abundant riches, not the least of which is eternal life. The Lord God swallows death and dries tears (Isa. 25:8). Those who waited for the Lord will look on Him in wonder, rejoicing in His redemption (v. 9). When Christ came He promised that the first would be last (Matt. 20:16). Paul taught that Christ took away the sting of death for the believer (1 Cor. 15:55–56). And the apostle John gave us song after glorious song of the redeemed praising the Lamb who was slain (see, for example, Rev. 5:9–10). We are to begin now. Our hearts fill with joy as we abide in Him (John 15:11). Can we say with the church, "Behold, this is our God" (Isa. 25:9) and wait in joyful expectation for that glorious day when death will be no more?

The remnant of Israel learned that Jerusalem itself was not their strong city, but rather the Lord God was, the one who keeps His people who trust in Him in perfect peace (Isa. 26:1–3). He makes level paths for the righteous, and they desire a relationship with Him (vv. 7–9). The zeal He has for His people is a witness to the nations, and His people finally acknowledge that He alone is their ruler. In faithfulness to His promise to Abraham, He enlarges the borders of the promised land so that people from every tribe, tongue, and nation will awake from the grave and sing for joy when the Lord returns to judge the living and the dead (vv. 15, 19). Christ's second coming from heaven would be terrifying apart from His atoning sacrifice on the cross of Calvary and His perfect life of obedience that He lived for God's people. When Christ comes, will His blood cover you? Neither the earth nor our belongings nor our family ties will save us. In Christ alone is where our faith must lie.

On the final day of the Lord, God will punish all evil, including Satan himself (Rev. 20:7–10). But His own children He will keep safe eternally. Earth and heaven will become one, and the redeemed, whose sins have been atoned for by the blood of Jesus, will fill the whole world (Isa. 27:6). The trumpet will sound, and peoples from Assyria, Israel, and Egypt, as well as a multitude of other nations, will come and worship in the New Jerusalem. Both the individual (we'll be gleaned one by one) and the corporate (we'll come together to worship) are emphasized here (vv. 12–13). Our individual names must be found in the Lamb's Book of Life, yet we come together as the multiethnic bride of Christ to sing praises to Him. How glorious that day will be!

❦ ❦ ❦ ❦

In what are you tempted to place your security today because of your great need? These chapters beckon us to turn to Christ and trust in Him, our Rock, forever. In Him we will find perfect peace as our minds are fixed on Him and our hearts trust in His Word. May our hearts yearn for Him and earnestly seek Him through the Scriptures.

May our daily song be,

> O LORD, You are my God.
> I will exalt You,
> I will praise Your name,
> For You have done wonderful things;
> Your counsels of old are faithfulness and truth.
> > (Isa. 25:1)

Processing It Together...

1. What do we learn about God in Isaiah 13–27?

2. How does this reshape how we should view our present circumstances?

3. What do we learn about God's Son, Jesus Christ?

4. How should this impact our relationship with God and with others?

5. What do we learn about God's covenant with His people?

6. How are we to live in light of this?

7. How can we apply Isaiah 13–27 to our lives today and in the future?

8. How should we apply this passage in our churches?

9. Look back at "Put It in Perspective" in your personal study questions. What did you find challenging or encouraging about this lesson?

10. Look back at "Principles and Points of Application." How has this lesson impacted your life?

A Remnant Will Be Redeemed

Isaiah 28–35

Purpose...

Head. What do I need to know from this passage in Scripture?

- The righteous King, ultimately Jesus Christ, redeems a remnant and makes them rejoice.

Heart. How does what I learn from this passage affect my internal relationship with the Lord?

- I am a kingdom disciple who has been redeemed so that I can walk in the way of holiness and find my security and strength in King Jesus.

Hands. How does what I learn from this passage translate into action for God's kingdom?

- I will sit under the preaching of the word of God at a gospel-centered church each Lord's Day.
- I will confidently engage and evangelize unbelievers, praying for the Lord to save them.
- I will let my worship of God be my greatest witness for God in my home, workplace, and neighborhood.
- I will encourage someone this week with the truth that God is ready to protect, spare, and rescue His people.

Personal Study...

Pray. Ask that God will open up your heart and mind as you study His Word. This is His story of redemption that He has revealed to us, and the Holy Spirit is our teacher.

Ponder the Passage. Read Isaiah 28–35. You may want to consider reading and answering questions on day 1 for chapter 28; on day 2 for chapter 29; on day 3 for chapter 30; on day 4 for chapters 31–32; on day 5 for chapters 33–35; and review or catch up on day 6.

- *Point.* What is the point of this passage? How does this relate to the point of the entire book?

- *Persons.* Who are the main people involved in this passage? What characterizes them?

- *Persons of the Trinity.* Where do you see God the Father, God the Son, and God the Holy Spirit in this passage?

- *Puzzling Parts.* Are there any parts of the passage that you don't quite understand or that seem interesting or confusing?

Put It in Perspective.

- *Place in Scripture.* What is the original context of this text? What is the redemptive-historical context—what has or hasn't happened in redemptive history at this point in Scripture? How does this text connect to Christ?

The following questions will help you if you got stuck on any of the previous questions and will help you dig a little deeper into the text, putting it all into perspective.

1. 28:1–6. (a) Who is being judged in these verses, and why?

(b) Who will be the Lord's instrument to destroy Ephraim (see 2 Kings 17:6)?

(c) Who is Ephraim's only hope?

2. 28:7–22. (a) Briefly describe the condition of the leadership in Jerusalem.

(b) How did the Lord rise up at Mount Perazim (see 2 Sam. 5:17–21) and in the Valley of Gibeon (see Josh. 10:1–11)?

(c) What is the point Paul is making when he uses verses 11–12 in 1 Corinthians 14:20–25?

(d) How does Paul use verse 16 in Romans 9:30–33? How does Peter use it in 1 Peter 2:4–6?

3. 28:23–29. (a) What questions regarding Jerusalem's future do these two parables provoke?

(b) How did Jesus, as the ultimate man of wisdom, use parables in His ministry?

4. 29:1–8. (a) It is likely that Ariel means "altar hearth" (see Ezek. 43:15–16). Why is this an appropriate nickname for Jerusalem (see Ps. 84:3–4; Isa. 6:4–7; 33:14)?

(b) Who has made it possible for us to stand in the presence of God, who is a consuming fire (see Heb. 4:14–16; 12:18–29)?

5. 29:9–16. (a) How do these verses reveal the danger of ignoring God's word?

(b) Why did Jesus use verse 13 in rebuking the Pharisees and scribes (see Matt. 15:1–9)?

(c) What is Paul saying when he uses verse 14 in 1 Corinthians 1:18–19?

6. 29:17–24. (a) God's grace is grounded in what (see Gen. 3:15; 12:1–3)?

(b) How does Jesus fulfill these verses (see Matt. 11:2–6)?

7. 30:1–17. (a) In whom are God's people tempted to put their trust?

(b) How has the Lord already shown Himself superior to this nation in redemptive history (see Ex. 14:1–15:21)?

8. 30:18–26. (a) What hope is there for the remnant of faithful believers?

(b) How do these verses anticipate Jesus's first coming (see Matt. 23:10), as well as His second coming, when He ushers in the new heavens and the new earth (see Rev. 21:22–22:5)?

9. 30:27–33. (a) How does judgment fall on the enemy of God's people?

(b) How do these verses anticipate the final day of judgment (see Rev. 19:11–21)?

10. 31:1–5. (a) How does Deuteronomy 17:14–20 inform your understanding of these verses?

(b) Compare verse 3 with John 4:24.

(c) How is verse 5 ultimately transformed by Christ (see Luke 13:31–35 and Rev. 21:2)?

11. 31:6–32:20. (a) According to verse 8, what is Assyria's future?

(b) Why are ease and complacency dangerous for God's people?

(c) When was 32:15 fulfilled (see Acts 2:1–21)?

12. 33:1–12. (a) How do these verses reveal both the judgment of God and His mercy?

(b) How do verses 5–6 find their fulfillment (see 1 Cor. 1:30)?

13. 33:13–24. (a) How does Isaiah portray the future of Zion in these verses?

(b) How is this picture fulfilled in the New Testament (see Heb. 12:22–29)?

14. 34:1–17. (a) What is the history of enmity between Edom and God's people, and how is Edom representative of anyone opposed to God (see Gen. 25:23; 33:4–16; Num. 20:14–21; 1 Sam. 14:47; 2 Sam. 8:14; 1 Kings 11:1–17, 23–25; 2 Kings 8:20; 14:7, 10; Ps. 137:7; Obad. 10–14)?

(b) How do these verses anticipate the final day of judgment (see Rev. 19:11–21 or question 9b above)?

15. 35:1–10. (a) How does Isaiah portray Zion's future?

(b) How does the author of Hebrews use verse 3 in 12:11–17?

(c) How do verses 5–6 anticipate Jesus's coming (see Matt. 11:5; John 7:37–39; Acts 3:1–10)?

(d) How does this chapter reveal the future reversal of Genesis 3:17–19 (see also Rom. 8:18–25)?

Principles and Points of Application

16. 28:1–29. (a) What are some of the ways you can make sure you hear the word of the Lord—each Sunday and on a daily basis?

(b) In what ways have you been tempted to compare yourself with others or with the world instead of examining yourself against Scripture? How are you tempted to pursue salvation (including sanctification) by works instead of by faith (see Rom. 9:30–33)?

17. **29:1–14.** (a) Give a couple examples of how we often draw near to God with our mouths while our hearts are far from Him. How could you use these examples to discuss true worship with your children or with a friend?

(b) Why is it encouraging as you engage and evangelize unbelievers to know that God has made man's wisdom to be foolishness (see 1 Cor. 1:18–21)?

18. **29:15–24.** (a) Give some examples of how sinners turn things upside down and disregard their Maker.

(b) How do you sanctify and stand in awe of the Holy God in your home, workplace, church, and community?

19. **30:1–33.** (a) Who or what are you seeking for direction and protection instead of the Lord? How do these verses challenge you?

(b) Memorize

> In returning and rest you shall be saved;
> In quietness and confidence shall be your strength. (30:15)

How will you apply this to your present circumstances?

20. **31:1–32:20.** (a) Why does it encourage you that the Spirit is poured on us (32:15)? How do verses such as 31:4–5 and 32:16–19 encourage you? What do they tell you about the Lord?

(b) In what area(s) of your life are you complacent? How is this dangerous to your spiritual health?

21. 33:1–35:10. (a) Why do you need the Lord to be "the stability of your times" (33:6)?

(b) Spend time in prayer for yourself, your family, and your church family, asking the Lord to strengthen you to walk righteously, speak uprightly, hear selectively, and see purely.

(c) Spend time in prayer for your unbelieving friends and neighbors, asking the Lord to give you opportunity to share the gospel with them that He might save them.

(d) In what ways are your heart anxious, your hands weak, and your knees feeble? How does chapter 35 encourage you to be strong and not fear?

(e) Reflect on 35:10. How can you and your family become more eternally minded?

Putting It All Together...

In shifting circumstances I always need the Lord to be my stability, but I often fail to look to Him first. Often, I want to put my trust in another person's word of comfort or wisdom. Sometimes I want to put my trust in resources, such as finances. It's when my heart is most anxious that my hand wants to grab for security from all the wrong places instead of finding my strength in trusting the Lord. Isn't this often the case for all of us? When the suffering is intensifying, the sin looming, or the service overwhelming, don't we often trust in the things that are made instead of in the Maker? These chapters in Isaiah challenge us to turn our anxious hearts to God for stability and salvation. The reigning King over the nations longs to reign in our hearts as well. He offers us fullness of joy in place of our faltering fingers and knocking knees. He offers us singing in place of cringing. And He offers us the way of holiness in place of sinfulness. He comes to turn that which is upside-down right side up, and He invites us to be a part of His plans and purposes as we proclaim His name to the nations.

I. A Remnant Will Be Redeemed (28–29)

As the Lord brings down the crown of pride of the drunkards of the Northern Kingdom and makes their glorious beauty fade underneath the mighty arm of the Assyrians, He raises His crown of glory for the remnant of His people. Only the humble people who look to Him will be saved by His strong arm (Isa. 28:5–6). The priest and the prophet who swallowed wine were in the end swallowed by it (v. 7). No longer able to understand the Lord's message, Israel was taken into captivity by the Assyrians (vv. 11–13).

Jerusalem should have learned their lesson. But instead, the people fooled themselves into thinking they were immune by believing lies and taking shelter in an alliance with Egypt (Isa. 28:14–15). This was the place to which the Lord God had told His people never to return because He had delivered them with His mighty power from Egypt in order to worship Him (Deut. 17:16). The sure foundation of such worship was the precious cornerstone He laid in Zion (Isa. 28:16), the city that represented His presence, promises, and protection, which is ultimately fulfilled in Jesus Christ (Rom. 9:30–33; 1 Peter 2:4–6). As Jerusalem watches the things in which they placed their security be swept away, they will be terrified (Isa. 28:17–19). Even the comfort of their own bed cannot pacify (v. 20). Just as the Lord gave the Philistines into David's hand on Mount Perazim (2 Sam. 5:17–21) and the Amorites into Joshua's hand (Josh. 10:1–11), so too He would rise up and give His people into the hand of the Assyrians (Isa. 28:21–22). In wisdom the Lord does excellently, even when it means judgment comes on His own people. The principle of sowing and reaping applies in the case of Israel. What they have sown in rebellion they reap in rejection, yet the Lord also gives grace. The remnant that rests in His righteousness will be saved (vv. 23–29).

The plummet, or plumb line, of righteousness has never changed throughout the course of redemptive history (Isa. 28:17). A person cannot be saved apart from fulfilling the precepts of the Lord. But how can sinful humanity do this? Scripture continually reminds us that we cannot fulfill the precepts of the Lord. Isaiah reveals that the key to salvation is the foundation in Zion that the Lord God has laid. The precious cornerstone, Christ Jesus, is both just and the justifier. The New Testament makes this clear. As Romans 3:25–26 says, "God set forth [Christ] as a propitiation by His blood, through faith, to demonstrate His righteousness, because in His forbearance God had passed over the sins that were previously committed, to demonstrate at the present time His righteousness, that He might be just and the justifier of the one who has faith in Jesus." The One who became wisdom from God has done excellently for God's people (1 Cor. 1:30). Those who are in Christ Jesus stand before the heavenly Father clothed in His righteousness (2 Cor. 5:21). He became righteousness for us (1 Cor. 1:30) and has declared us not guilty (Rom. 8:31–34). In light of such a salvation, we are to stop making lies our refuge, taking shelter in falsehood, and hiding in bed. We are to look to our crown of glory and diadem of beauty, walking in His counsel and wisdom by studying His precepts.

Jerusalem symbolized the presence, promises, and protection of God amid His people because His temple was there. And in the temple the sacrifices on the altar were kept burning continually. On the one hand, this represented humanity's greatest hope and comfort—atonement for sin. On the other hand, it represented humanity's greatest fear—judgment because of sin. Jerusalem had to choose. Would the people take God as their comfort and hope, or would they reject the God who could save them and be consumed by His fire of judgment? Their outward performance didn't fool God. Hearts amiss lead to heads and hands that miss the mark of true worship. The city that was to be a light to the nations would now be judged by the nations (Isa. 29:1–10). They chose to close their eyes to the things of God and look to a human who couldn't save them. But the Lord cannot forsake His promises, and He will again do wonderful things with the people He has chosen (v. 14). He will make the wisdom of the age perish and raise up the wisest one of all, His own Son, Jesus Christ. He too wept over Jerusalem (Luke 13:34). He makes our hearts new so that we can worship God in spirit and in truth. He has opened our eyes that were closed and softened our hearts to save us from sin so that we can live for Him.

Those who had been set apart as God's people had turned from Him, thinking they could run their own lives without Him seeing or knowing what they were doing (Isa. 29:15). But the Maker knows those He has made, and they can't hide from Him. Thankfully, the scoffer will not have the final say. The Redeemer of Abraham will yet again redeem a remnant for Himself (v. 22). He will turn things right side up (vv. 17–21)! Shame will be turned to sanctification of God's great name (v. 23). The Lord will bring the wayward to understanding and the grumblers to submission. Righting the world will mean sending the righteous One. Jesus became to us sanctification from God so that we can stand in awe of the God of Israel (1 Cor. 1:30). The redeemed are to join together as the work of God's hands and worship Him, work for His glory, and witness to the nations of God's great name.

II. A Righteous King Will Reign (30–32)

One of the desperate pleas of our hearts as God's children should be, "Not my will, but Yours be done." It's a plea of dependence on the Lord, who knows what is best for us. Here we see how rebellious Israel's heart had become. Instead of trusting in the Lord who had made a covenant with them, they make an alliance with Egypt (Isa. 30:1–2). Instead of repenting, they further rebel. Instead of asking for God's direction, they direct their steps to Pharaoh. Sadly, Isaiah can see what Israel can't. The journey to Egypt will be filled with danger, and it will gain them nothing in the end (vv. 3–5). They put their trust in a nation who sits still instead of in the Holy One of Israel, who moves through history raising up and putting down nations at His command (vv. 6–7).

Israel's rejection of God's word was costly, as all sin proves to be (Isa. 30:8–17). Yet the Lord extended grace to them (vv. 18–33). If they would return and rest in His salvation, then they would find strength. Through adversity and affliction He would teach the remnant to hear His word and walk in His ways (v. 21). Darkness would give way to light and brokenness to beauty. The Holy One of Israel will sift His people from the nations, and they will run to the rock (v. 29). The Assyrians will become as nothing before the Lord's victorious power (v. 31).

Jesus came as the teacher who, through faith, people saw, heard, and believed. He came to be gracious to us, and the Father exalted Him to show mercy to His people. In justice He poured out His wrath on His own Son so that we can be saved. In turning and resting in Jesus, we will be saved. Yet how we long for easy alliances like Israel had with Egypt. We want to secure our own salvation from our troubles because we don't like to wait for the Lord. Yet He waits to be gracious to us, if only we would turn to Him, the rock of our redemption.

The covenant Lord set certain rules for Israel regarding kingship. They weren't to have just any king. They were to set the king of the Lord's choosing over them. And this king was not to return to Egypt to acquire horses or for any other reason because it would turn his heart away from the true God (Deut. 17:14–17). Yet in Hezekiah's day, Israel made an alliance with Egypt, cowering beneath the looming Assyrians (Isa. 31:1). How foolish to put their trust in humankind and horses instead of in God, who is a spirit. Far greater than horses coming up from Egypt would be the Lord of hosts coming down to fight on Mount Zion in order to protect His city from the invading Assyrian army (vv. 4–5). No nation can stand before the sword of the Lord. His motive for protecting Jerusalem is tied to kingship. He had chosen the city of David for the king of His choosing, which is ultimately Jesus Christ. But God's people weren't ready for His powerful works or prophetic word. Women were complacent, thinking everything was going on as normal when actually society around them was crumbling (32:9–20). But the Lord had a day when He would pour out His Spirit, and justice and righteousness would usher in peace and quietness.

Following His death, resurrection, and exaltation, Jesus sent the gift of His Spirit to God's people. Those who live according to the Spirit experience life and peace (Rom. 8:6) as they look to King Jesus, the righteous king who reigns on the throne of thrones awaiting the day when He will return to gather His people and usher them into the most peaceful habitation of all with secure dwellings and quiet resting places in the new heavens and the new earth. What a blessed day that will be! How are you living in light of this day now, experiencing life and peace because you have set your mind on the Spirit of God and on eternity?

III. A Redeemed People Will Rejoice (33–35)

God's people cowered under the threat of Assyria, misplacing their trust in Egypt instead of trusting in the mighty arm of the covenant Lord. But in the final of six woes in chapters 28–35, we learn that the Lord will destroy Assyria (33:1–24). The mighty King-Warrior rises up to protect His people and keep His promises. The enemy will not have the final word. The covenant Lord will fill Zion with justice and righteousness, bringing salvation, wisdom, and knowledge to His people. Those who shake their hands, stop their ears, and shut their eyes from evil will behold the beauty of the majestic king. The lawgiver is also the love giver. The Judge is also the Savior. Sin and sickness will be no more.

Jesus came to those waiting for the redemption of Jerusalem (Luke 2:38). He came to be the mighty arm of salvation. He arose from the grave, lifted Himself up, and was exalted at the right hand of God the Father. In the New Jerusalem, our greatest joy will be beholding our king. There our Lord will be before us in majesty. The Judge of all the earth will save us because He has atoned for our sins. With sin and sickness removed, the curse will give way to the blessing of the new heavens and the new earth, in which we will reign with Him forever.

As blessed as the New Jerusalem will be for God's people, the curse of judgment will be severe for all who refuse to look to Him as king (Isa. 34:1–17). The Lord's wrath is on all who trust in anyone or anything but Him. Edom, a long-standing enemy of Israel's, was defeated only by King David (2 Sam. 8:13–14), but there is coming a day when the greater and final Davidic king, Jesus Christ, will defeat all God's enemies. The Lord has a day of vengeance in which He will lay waste the possessions and people not His own. Jesus will return with a sword to strike down the nations. The King of kings and Lord of lords will lead the armies of heaven as He comes to pour out God's wrath on the nations (Rev. 19:13–16). Such knowledge should lead us to pray for the lost, engaging them with the gospel and asking the Lord to save them. There is no other name under heaven that can save us. Jesus will either be beautiful for us to behold, or He will be a terror from which we will want to flee. Today is the day of salvation. If you've never placed your trust in Christ, turn to Him today in repentance and faith.

For those who know Christ, eternity awaits, in which we will see the glory of the Lord and the majesty of God (Isa. 35:1–2). But already Christ has come and shown us the glory of the Father (John 1:14). He has opened blind eyes and made the deaf hear and the lame leap. The waters of eternal life flow from His Spirit, who is given to all who believe in Christ. Those who have new hearts and therefore walk in the way of holiness must constantly strengthen weak hands and knees and hearts, taking courage in the Lord our God who has redeemed us and has glory in store for us (Isa. 35:3–4; Heb. 12:12–13). Already we have joy in Christ (John 15:11). In the New Jerusalem we will have eternal joy. Sorrow, sighing, and sin will be gone, and we will be in the presence of our blessed Lord and Savior Jesus Christ forever.

In what shifting circumstances do you need the Lord to be your stability today? What suffering is intensifying, sin looming, or service overwhelming? Turn your anxious heart to the Lord today for stability and salvation. The reigning King over the nations longs to reign in your heart. He offers you fullness of joy in place of your faltering fingers and knocking knees. He offers you singing in place of cringing. And He offers you the way of holiness in place of sinfulness. He has come to turn that which is upside-down right side up, including our own lives. And He invites us to be a part of His mission by praising Him; pouring out our time, talents, and treasures for Him; and proclaiming His name to the nations.

Processing It Together...

1. What do we learn about God in Isaiah 28–35?

2. How does this reshape how we should view our present circumstances?

3. What do we learn about God's Son, Jesus Christ?

4. How should this impact our relationship with God and with others?

5. What do we learn about God's covenant with His people?

6. How are we to live in light of this?

7. How can we apply Isaiah 28–35 to our lives today and in the future?

8. How should we apply this passage in our churches?

9. Look back at "Putting It in Perspective" in your personal study questions. What did you find challenging or encouraging about this lesson?

10. Look back at "Principles and Points of Application." How has this lesson transformed your life?

Now in Whom Do You Trust?

Isaiah 36–37

Purpose...

Head. What do I need to know from this passage in Scripture?

- The Lord God is worthy of our trust because He defends His people for His own sake and the sake of His servant David, who is ultimately Jesus Christ.

Heart. How does what I learn from this passage affect my internal relationship with the Lord?

- I am a kingdom disciple who trusts in the Lord God, maker of heaven and earth.

Hands. How does what I learn from this passage translate into action for God's kingdom?

- I will help those facing distress and disgrace to put their trust in the Lord alone.

- I will pray for the Lord to display His glory in the lives of my family and church family so that others might know that He alone is Lord.

- I will share with others how the Lord has delivered me from sin and suffering, exalting His name.

Personal Study...

Pray. Ask that God will open up your heart and mind as you study His Word. This is His story of redemption that He has revealed to us, and the Holy Spirit is our teacher.

Ponder the Passage. Read Isaiah 36–37. See also 2 Kings 18:13–19:37.

- *Point.* What is the point of this passage? How does this relate to the point of the entire book?

- *Persons.* Who are the main people involved in this passage? What characterizes them?

- *Persons of the Trinity.* Where do you see God the Father, God the Son, and God the Holy Spirit in this passage?

- *Puzzling Parts.* Are there any parts of the passage that you don't quite understand or that seem interesting or confusing?

Put It in Perspective.

- *Place in Scripture.* What is the original context of this text? What is the redemptive-historical context—what has or hasn't happened in redemptive history at this point in Scripture? How does this text connect to Christ?

The following questions will help you if you got stuck on any of the previous questions, and they will help you dig a little deeper into the text, putting it all into perspective.

1. **36:1–10.** (a) Where is the place the Assyrian military officer stood, and why is it significant (see 7:3; 22:9–11)?

   (b) The word "trust" recurs in verses 4–9. Why is this significant for this section as well as for the sections of the book you've studied so far?

   (c) In what ways does the Assyrian military officer try to place doubt and fear in the minds of God's people, and what elements of truth are in his words?

   (d) Look back at 28:11–15. How has this prophecy come true?

(e) How do John 12:36; 14:1; and Romans 15:13 answer, "What confidence is this in which you trust?"

2. 36:11–21. (a) Why would it be disastrous for the people on the wall to hear the Assyrian military officer?

(b) How did the Assyrian military officer try to place doubt and fear about Hezekiah's kingship in the people's minds?

(c) How did he try to place doubt and fear about the Lord's kingship?

(d) How is the people's response a sign of Hezekiah's (and ultimately the Lord's) great leadership?

(e) Who is ultimately behind the taunts of the Assyrians (see Luke 4:1–13; John 8:44), and how are such taunts overcome (see 1 John 2:28–29)?

3. 36:22–37:7. (a) What is Hezekiah's concern regarding the people's response to the Assyrian military officer's words?

(b) From whom and for whom does Hezekiah request prayer?

(c) What word of comfort does the Lord give Hezekiah through Isaiah?

(d) Use a concordance to get an idea of how many times the Lord says, "Do not be afraid," or something similar (for example, "Do not fear"; "Do not worry") in the book of Isaiah and then in Scripture as a whole.

4. **37:8–13.** (a) According to verses 8–9a, why does Assyria depart from attacking Judah?

(b) How does the Assyrian king try to cast doubt on Hezekiah's faith this time?

(c) How do these taunts anticipate Matthew 27:37–44?

5. **37:14–20.** (a) How does Hezekiah's response differ from his earlier response in 37:1–2?

(b) What is Hezekiah's motivation for praying what he prays, and how does this reflect Exodus 19:4–6 and Deuteronomy 4:5–8?

(c) Ultimately, when and how will all the kingdoms of the earth know that the God of Israel alone is Lord (skim Revelation 18–22)?

6. **37:21–35.** (a) What was the effect of Hezekiah's prayer?

(b) How does the Lord return Assyria's evil on its own head?

(c) What do you learn about the *remnant* in these verses?

(d) The remnant is a theme that stretches from Genesis to Revelation. What do you learn about this remnant from the following verses: Genesis 45:4–8; Ezra 9:8–15; Nehemiah 1:1–3; Acts 15:13–17; Romans 9:27–29; 11:1–10?

(e) How is verse 35 ultimately fulfilled?

7. **37:36–38.** (a) Read 14:24–27. How do 37:36–38 fill in details?

(b) What does this incident anticipate (see Rev. 19:11–21)?

Principles and Points of Application

8. **36:1–21.** (a) On what are you resting your trust instead of in the Lord alone? Spend time in confession and repentance, asking the Lord to help you trust Him only.

(b) Who or what has cast doubt in your heart and mind regarding God's power to deliver you? How do these verses challenge you to respond?

9. **36:22–37:7.** Think of someone you know who is facing a day of distress and disgrace. Spend time praying for the Lord to strengthen them.

10. **37:8–38.** (a) Perhaps you thought you had conquered a sin in your life or you believed your physical suffering was over, only to have it return. How were you tempted toward discouragement and defeat? How do these verses encourage you to fight feelings of despair with faith?

(b) Use Hezekiah's prayer in verses 16–20 to write out your own prayer to God regarding your specific circumstances.

(c) How does the rerouting of the Assyrian king and the Lord sparing Jerusalem bolster your trust in Him for your circumstances?

Putting It All Together...

I wasn't intending to apply for the position, but when it came available I felt compelled by the Holy Spirit to do so, and my husband was encouraging and supportive. But after I applied and was asked for an interview, I felt a mixture of excitement and fear. In the excited moments, I really wanted to use my gifts to serve in this job. In the fearful moments, I wondered how in the world I could work and raise four children at the same time. I continually had to get on my knees because the issue for me during those days was one of trust. *In whom do you now trust, Sarah? Do you trust in your own giftedness and networking and the favor of interviewers, or do you trust in the Lord your God who moves the hearts of people as easily as we move pawns in a game?* This lesson is timely for us all because it's a lesson about trust. On what or on whom do we rest our trust? Oftentimes the answer is God *and* something or someone else—the doctor, the relationship, the contact, or the bank account. Rarely do we rest in God *alone*.

These two chapters are like a penetrating gaze. They force you to examine your heart to see where you're placing your trust. They also demonstrate in a profound way what we just learned in the last lesson. The Lord is "wonderful in counsel and excellent in guidance" (Isa. 28:29). "In returning and rest" is salvation, and "in quietness and confidence" is our strength (30:15). The Lord is gracious and merciful to "those who wait for Him" (30:18). The Lord of hosts will defend, deliver, and preserve Jerusalem (31:5). He is His people's salvation "in the time of trouble" (33:2). He rises to the occasion and exalts Himself above all so-called gods (33:10). And He comes with vengeance on His enemies in order to save His own; therefore, God's people don't have to fear (35:4).

I. Now in Whom Do You Trust? (36:1–37:7)

If you've ever been caught in a dangerous storm, you know the fear of having no place to turn. Sennacherib, king of Assyria, was that storm who came whirling against Judah in 701 BC.[1] After defeating all the fortified cities of Judah, he set his eyes on Jerusalem.

---

1. Hezekiah's fourteenth year doesn't match with the date of Sennacherib's invasion (701 BC), so commentators have proposed several solutions, two of which are most likely. Either there is a copyist error

At the place where the Lord had spoken to Hezekiah's father, Ahaz, through the prophet Isaiah, calling him not to fear and to put his faith in the Lord God and where Ahaz had failed to trust, the Assyrian military officer stood to declare war (Isa. 36:2). In whom would Hezekiah trust? Would he trust in the Lord God, or would he go the way of his father and trust in the kingdoms of this world? The military officer tried hard to unsettle Hezekiah's leaders, who would relay the message to King Hezekiah. He questioned the place and person in whom they trusted (vv. 4–10). There are certainly elements of truth to his argument. For example, he challenged Judah's misplaced trust in Egypt. But he mistakenly assumed that Judah's God was like one of his gods. He failed to recognize that Judah's God is the only living and true God, and therefore he offered false trust in the king of Assyria.

Understandably, Hezekiah's leaders who were listening were unsettled when the officer spoke in the common language of the people, especially since he was within earshot of the people on the city wall (Isa. 36:11). What if they trembled in fear and fled? But this was exactly the Assyrian officer's tactic. He wanted to instill fear in God's people. So he lifted his voice even louder and addressed them with the authority of the great king of Assyria (vv. 13–20). His first tactic was to raise doubt in King Hezekiah's ability to lead and deliver them. If he could get them to stop following their king, then they would be more likely to follow the king of Assyria. Second, he tried to raise their doubt in the Lord's ability to deliver them. If he could get them to recognize the totality of destruction that the king of Assyria had left in his wake with surrounding nations, then maybe they would place their allegiance elsewhere. Finally, to make matters a bit sweeter, he promised that from the time of their allegiance to the time of deportation, things would go well for them regarding provision of food and land. But the people didn't take the bait; instead, they were silent, just as Hezekiah had instructed them to be (v. 21).

These encounters between the enemy and the people of God began with the fall in the garden in Genesis 3 and stretch to the book of Revelation. In between, Christ's life, death, and resurrection sounded a climactic note of victory. Jesus overcame the devil's temptations in the wilderness (Luke 4:1–15) and disarmed principalities and powers, triumphing over them in the cross of Calvary (Col. 2:15), even though the devil tried to get Jesus to place His trust in anyone and anything other than His Father. Jesus was silent, as a sheep led to the slaughter, looking to His Father in the time of greatest suffering. Working in tandem with the world and our own flesh, this tempter comes to us too. He wants to sow seeds of doubt in God's trustworthiness when our dreams are dashed, our marriage is in distress, our childless arms remain unfilled, our chronic pain is at its worst, the child who once professed Christ turns elsewhere, our parents who were faithful in ministry lose their memory, or the job we coveted and attained crumbles. Will we be silent, trusting in the Lord's sovereignty? Or will we cry out against Him, turning our trust to another relationship or other methods, means,

here and it should have read twenty-fourth year, or Hezekiah ruled with his father, Ahaz, until 715 BC, making 701 BC the fourteenth year of his solo reign.

or money? The Lord will deliver us. You can bank on that truth. The question today is, "Now in whom do you trust?" (Isa. 36:5).

You can imagine the king's leaders tearing their clothes in distress and disgrace (Isa. 36:22). Hezekiah too tore his clothes in distress at the news (37:1). It was a day of disgrace for God's people. Imagine carrying a baby for nine months and then not having the strength to push him or her out (v. 3). But Hezekiah, unlike Ahaz his father, turned to the right place and, more importantly, the right person. He went to the temple, the place that symbolized God's presence, promises, and protection. And he asked for prayer. He sent his leaders to the prophet Isaiah to ask for prayer for the remnant (vv. 2–4). Throughout Scripture we see that the Lord God always preserves a remnant of His people to worship Him (see, for example, Gen. 45:4–8; Ezra 9:8–15; Neh. 1:1–3; Acts 15:13–17; Rom. 9:27–29; 11:1–10). As long as redemptive history continues, there will always be a remnant in the midst of unbelievers to worship Him, work for His glory, and witness to others concerning His great name. The Lord sent a powerful word of truth to Hezekiah to encourage him to stand firm in his faith. He should not be afraid of the enemy's words because the Lord would fill him with fear, turn his footsteps away from Jerusalem, and make him fall by his own sword. The command not to fear happens often in Isaiah (see, for example, 8:12; 35:4; 41:10, 13; 43:1; 51:7; 54:4), but it's also a recurring theme throughout Scripture (see, for example, Deut. 1:29; Josh. 1:9; 1 Chron. 28:20; Ps. 27:1; Matt. 10:28; 1 Cor. 16:13). Because God is for us and Christ is interceding for us and Christ's Spirit is in us, nothing can separate us from God's love in Christ (Rom. 8:31–39). Nothing—not the broken engagement, unfaithful husband, tragic death of a loved one, cancer, or financial ruin. And not the monotonous moments in which we're tempted to drift from faithfulness. Now in whom do you trust?

II. We Trust in the Lord Our God (37:8–38)

On his return from speaking to Hezekiah's officials, the Rabshakeh (the Assyrian official) learned that Sennacherib had changed his planned attack on Jerusalem to fight against the Cushites. Whether the Cushites had really set out to fight against him isn't certain, but the Lord used this word to turn Sennacherib away from His holy city. But Sennacherib wasn't through with Hezekiah. He sought to undermine Hezekiah's faith in God by accusing Him of being deceptive and by boasting in his record of destroying other nations (Isa. 37:10–13). Now in whom did Hezekiah trust?

Again, Hezekiah went to the house of the Lord, but this time he didn't send a message to Isaiah to pray for the remnant. Instead, he got on his knees and spread out the letter from Sennacherib before God (Isa. 37:14–20). First, he acknowledged God as King of all kings, the one living and true God, and the creator of all (v. 16). Second, he recognized Sennacherib was mocking God (v. 17). Third, he recognized the power of the Assyrians was great, but it was nothing in comparison to God's power (vv. 18–19). Fourth, he recognized God as the only source of salvation (v. 20a). Finally, his motive was missions—that all the kingdoms of the earth would know Judah's God alone is the Lord (v. 20b).

When we are ridiculed for our faith, we can be sure Jesus was ridiculed more. When the father of lies tries to convince us that God is not good, we should remember Jesus fought such lies with Scripture and do the same. And when we are up against powerful foes, we should fight from our knees like our Lord did, asking the Father to show His glory for the entire world to see.

Because Hezekiah prayed, the Lord responded (Isa. 37:21). The Lord always responds when His people pray. This word bolstered Hezekiah's faith in three main ways. First, the king of Assyria would not have the upper hand (v. 22). Jerusalem was safe because it was the Lord's. Second, the king of Assyria was no match for the powerful and Holy God of Israel (vv. 23–25). Finally, Assyria's doom was sure. God would put a hook in the nose of the nation that put hooks in other nations' noses and led them into captivity, and He would reroute them away from His city (vv. 26–29).

The sign that this word was true was an agricultural one, but it pointed to the reality of the remnant that the Lord would save (Isa. 37:30–32). The fruitfulness of vineyards symbolized the fruitfulness of the vine (Israel). A remnant would spring forth from Zion because of the zeal of the Lord. His anger was aroused against Assyria to be sure, but the ultimate reason He protected Zion was because of His servant David (v. 35). The Lord had made a covenant with David concerning an eternal kingdom with an eternal Davidic King (2 Samuel 7). In Christ this covenant finds its complete fulfillment. He is the King of all kings whose kingdom never ends. Even now believers "have come to Mount Zion and to the city of the living God, the heavenly Jerusalem… to Jesus the Mediator of the new covenant." (Heb. 12:22, 24).

The Lord's word was faithful and true. The angel of the Lord struck down in one night 185,000 Assyrians (Isa. 37:36). Sennacherib returned home and twenty years later was assassinated by his sons in his place of worship (vv. 37–38). This story is a microcosm of the ultimate day of judgment. For the sake of His servant David, Jesus Christ, the Lord will protect all those in the New Jerusalem from distress, disgrace, and destruction. Those who worship false gods will be condemned to spend an eternity in hell, but those who place their trust in the Lord God will live forever in the Holy City, where there will be no need for protection against advancing Assyrians because the Lord God has saved a people for His own sake and they are secure.

Reading these chapters was good for me during those days of waiting for the interview process to be over. Would I get the job, or did the Lord have someone else in mind for that position? It boiled down to a simple question of trust. Did I truly believe that the Lord had my best interest at heart and knew exactly what He was doing with me and where He wanted me? Did I trust in Him alone to bring about the plans for my life? Or was I trusting in my own abilities, achievements, networking, and resources, thinking those things would make or break it for me? The same God who rerouted Sennacherib could certainly route the hearts of the interviewers. If I was God's candidate for the job, then the Lord would open wide the door. In quietness and in trust I gained strength during those long days of waiting for the Lord's plan. This too is where your strength will come from as you wait for that phone call, test result, healed relationship, eased physical pain, job opening, or converted spouse or child. Let it be said when others look at your life, "She trusts in the Lord her God."

Processing It Together...

1. What do we learn about God in Isaiah 36–37?

2. How does this reshape how we should view our present circumstances?

3. What do we learn about God's Son, Jesus Christ?

4. How should this impact our relationship with God and with others?

5. What do we learn about God's covenant with His people?

6. How are we to live in light of this?

7. How can we apply Isaiah 36–37 to our lives today and in the future?

8. How should we apply this passage in our churches?

9. Look back at "Putting It in Perspective" in your personal study questions. What did you find challenging or encouraging about this lesson?

10. Look back at "Principles and Points of Application." How has this lesson impacted your life?

Deliverance and Declaration

Isaiah 38–39

Purpose...

Head. What do I need to know from this passage in Scripture?

- The Lord delivered Hezekiah's life and declared the future Babylonian exile, which revealed the need for a greater king than Hezekiah.

Heart. How does what I learn from this passage affect my internal relationship with the Lord?

- I am a kingdom disciple who has received salvation from the Lord, which means I have a new heart from which to sing praises to Him all the days of my life.

Hands. How does what I learn from this passage translate into action for God's kingdom?

- I will encourage a friend fearful of death with the truth that the Lord has numbered our days.
- I will seize opportunities to share the truth of God's love in Christ Jesus with someone this week.
- I will pass the faith to the next generation and teach them to sing of God's salvation daily.
- I will help others trust in the Lord alone instead of in their talents and treasures.
- I will look for ways to serve others before myself this week.

Personal Study...

Pray. Ask that God will open up your heart and mind as you study His Word. This is His story of redemption that He has revealed to us, and the Holy Spirit is our teacher.

Ponder the Passage. Read Isaiah 38–39. See also 2 Kings 20:1–19.

- *Point.* What is the point of this passage? How does this relate to the point of the entire book?
- *Persons.* Who are the main people involved in this passage? What characterizes them?
- *Persons of the Trinity.* Where do you see God the Father, God the Son, and God the Holy Spirit in this passage?
- *Puzzling Parts.* Are there any parts of the passage that you don't quite understand or that seem interesting or confusing?

Put It in Perspective.

- *Place in Scripture.* What is the original context of this text? What is the redemptive-historical context—what has or hasn't happened in redemptive history at this point in Scripture? How does this text connect to Christ?

The following questions will help you if you got stuck on any of the previous questions, and they will help you dig a little deeper into the text, putting it all into perspective.

1. **38:1–8.** (a) The events in these chapters precede the events in chapters 36–37. Based on what you learned in the last lesson and thinking ahead to the rest of the book of Isaiah, why does it make good sense for these chapters to be out of chronological sequence?

   (b) Does Hezekiah's prayer look to God's grace *alone*? Why or why not?

   (c) According to verse 5, on what does the Lord establish His grace (see also 2 Sam. 7:1–17)?

(d) How was verse 6 fulfilled (see 37:33–38)?

(e) What does the sign reveal about the Lord?

(f) What is the relationship between good works and faith, according to the New Testament (see Rom. 1:16–17; 3:21–27; 4:4–8; 6:23; James 2:14–26)?

2. **38:9–20.** (a) What does the writing of Hezekiah reveal regarding what he learned about the Lord during his illness and deliverance?

(b) According to verse 20, what was Hezekiah committed to doing for the extra fifteen years of his life?

(c) How is Christ our ultimate pledge of safety, and how has He made it possible for the Father to cast all our sins behind His back (see Heb. 9:11–14, 26; 10:14)?

3. **38:21–22.** (a) Since these verses are embedded in the parallel narrative in 2 Kings 20:7–8 but are separated here and placed immediately before 39:1, what purpose do you think they serve in this context?

(b) How did Hezekiah differ from his father, Ahaz (see Isa. 7:10–14)?

4. **39:1–8.** (a) How does the narrative hint that the men from Babylon did not just come to give Hezekiah a gift because they were glad he was better but had political intentions?

(b) How did Hezekiah respond, and why was this shameful in light of all that had transpired in the events recorded in chapter 38?

(c) Does Hezekiah seem to fear Isaiah's questions, or does he seem to have been glad he showed the men all that was in his storehouses? Give a reason for your answer.

(d) What is Babylon symbolic of in Scripture (see Gen. 11:1–9 and Rev. 18:2–8)?

(e) How does this prophecy give perspective to 37:34–38 and prepare us for the following chapters?

(f) How does Hezekiah's response to Isaiah reveal a self-centered heart? Contrast this with his response to the Lord's word through Isaiah in 38:2–3.

(g) How does this passage anticipate the choice a person must make between this world and Christ (see 1 John 2:15–17)?

Principles and Points of Application
  5. **38:1–8.** (a) How does it encourage you in your present circumstances that the Lord has numbered the days and years of our lives? How could you use this truth to encourage a friend this week?

(b) For what situation do you need to turn to the Lord in prayer, basing your request on His grace alone and resting in His answer?

(c) What is the greatest sign God the Father has given us to display His love for us and His faithfulness to fulfill His promises (see John 3:16–21)?

6. **38:9–22.** (a) Write out a prayer to the Lord, expressing your suffering, sin, and weariness in service, as well as your song of joy for the salvation He's given to you.

(b) How are you teaching those under your leadership to daily sing psalms and hymns and spiritual songs? Meditate on Colossians 3:16 this week, asking the Lord to give you opportunities to train others to fill their minds with God's word so their mouths can praise Him with hearts full of thanksgiving.

7. **39:1–8.** (a) In what way(s) are you tempted to display your time, talents, and treasures before others, hoping to gain success or significance in their eyes?

(b) Confess the ways you've been self-centered this week, asking the Lord to give you a heart that puts others first.

Putting It All Together...

With the help of social media and the internet, it seems so easy to trust in networking and the promotion of materials for our success, significance, and security instead of in the Lord alone. If only we could get enough "likes," then our product would be profitable. If only we could get So-and-So to endorse our work, then it would sell better. If only our children achieved better grades and increased in athletic ability, then we'd be favored too. The list is endless. Think about what you're most tempted to depend on for success and then how you go about achieving it. Do you really believe that the Lord is trustworthy, or do you keep Him in the background while taking things into your own hands, parading your product or personhood before others in order to gain their attention and favor? None of us are immune to this temptation. It is the way of the fallen human heart. We want to be great in others' eyes, and we're willing to show all that we have in order to achieve such significance. But the redeemed are called to something greater; indeed, we're called to Someone greater. Our success, significance, and security are in Christ alone. In this lesson we learn about the danger of becoming self-focused instead of remaining faithful to the King of kings.

I. The Lord Delivers Hezekiah's Life (38:1–22)

If the book of Isaiah had ended in the last chapter, we might have been tempted to put our trust in human kings, such as Hezekiah. After all, we saw great spiritual growth occur in Hezekiah's life, and chapter 37 ended on a climactic note. The Lord wins! Assyria falls! But for the book to close at chapter 37 would be shortsighted. We have learned in chapters 1–37 that the Lord is King of the nations and that He's saving a remnant for Himself, but we have also seen how faithless and fickle His people can be. How will He save them and secure His redemption of them? Chapters 38–39, although chronologically occurring before chapters 36–37, remind us that we cannot trust a human king and that our hearts are faithless and fickle. But they also prepare us for all that is to come in the remainder of the book, especially chapters 40–55, which are filled with prophecies of the Babylonian exile that occurred in three deportations (605, 597 and 586 BC) for the Southern Kingdom of Judah.

In 702 BC Hezekiah faced a life-threatening illness and was informed by Isaiah that it was the Lord's time for him to die.[1] But Hezekiah didn't want to die, so he pleaded with the Lord to preserve his life (Isa. 38:2–3). Hezekiah's prayer was not theologically correct. He pleaded for preservation based on his performance. And the Lord corrected this by His response (vv. 4–8). He completely ignored the perfect record Hezekiah set before Him and instead told Hezekiah of His own perfect record by stating that He is the God of David. It was because of His covenant promise to David (see 2 Sam. 7:1–17) that He would be gracious to Hezekiah and add fifteen years to his life. Not only this, but He would deliver Hezekiah (personally) and Jerusalem (nationally) from the king of Assyria. The Lord God would defend His city that represented His presence, protection, and promises. By a supernatural sign involving the sun, the Lord would confirm His sovereignty and creatorship to Hezekiah.

The psalm Hezekiah penned preserves his innermost thoughts during those days of sickness, and as such is a source of comfort to all those going through suffering (Isa. 38:9–20). It begins with Hezekiah's despair (vv. 10–15). In the midst of the roaring lions of suffering, the Lord is our only safety. Hezekiah also faced bitterness in his soul, recognizing God had chosen sickness for his lot. But because he recognized that God was sovereign over his sickness, he was quick to plead with Him to let him live (v. 16). Hezekiah also recognized that suffering had strengthened his faith, and for that he was grateful (v. 17a). He realized God's love was behind His sovereign plans, and as one who had been delivered from death to life, he would sing of the Lord's salvation all his days (vv. 17b–20).

---

1. This reckoning considers 687 to be the year Hezekiah died and the fifteen years in 38:5 as an exact figure. This also fits with the dates of Merodach-Baladan's (see 39:1) attempt for power between 705 and 702, which was squelched by King Sennacherib of Assyria. Motyer, *Prophecy of Isaiah*, 291, 296.

We also learn, after reading the psalm, that the Lord had provided an act (a cake of figs being applied to Hezekiah's boil) as well as a sign in response to Hezekiah's request for one (the sun turning back on the dial) (38:21). This entire chapter is meant to bring us to a grand conclusion: Hezekiah has seen the goodness of the Lord, and he has responded to it with a firm commitment to sing of God's goodness in the house of the Lord all the days of his life. We are also brought to the climactic expectation that this good king is going to be great for Judah, but our expectations are dashed with the record of the events in chapter 39, which point us forward to a far better king.

If chapter 38 emphasizes one thing, it's that salvation is by grace alone through faith alone. In his desperation, Hezekiah tried to bargain with God. "See how great I am! Look what I've done for You! Don't You want to keep me on Your team for awhile longer? Surely You're not yet done with me, a faithful, wholehearted king, are You?" But we cannot bargain with the Lord. His covenant of grace is secured by His own faithfulness. Jesus Christ is our pledge of safety from the wrath of God that will come to every sinner not clothed in the righteousness of Christ. The Father can cast all our sins behind His back because He poured them out on His Son on the cross. In love He has delivered our life from the pit of destruction because He chose us in Christ before the foundation of the world. He has extended eternal life to us so that we might pass the faith to the next generation and sing praises to Him all our days. Whether we are suffering from an extreme illness, a troubled marriage, or financial crisis, or whether we are suffering from the monotony of a daily routine that never seems to change, the Lord calls us to something greater than despair by delivering us to life in His Son, giving us joy-filled hearts that overflow with songs.

II. The Lord Declares the Babylonian Exile (39:1–8)

To Hezekiah, the king who had experienced God's love, words, deliverance, and sign/act and committed to pass on the faith to the next generation and play music in God's house all the days of his life, came temptation. Don't ever believe that you're above the world, the flesh, and the devil tempting you. No matter how close you're walking with the Lord, you must always be on your guard. Assyria had been the dominating force of the day, but there were rebellions against the kings of Assyria. One such rebellion was led by Merodach-Baladan, the son of Babylon's king. Sending letters and a present to Hezekiah was advantageous to him. He didn't need Hezekiah to help him, but surely he'd be glad for any help in rebelling against Sennacherib. Hezekiah was only too eager to help him. Showing Merodach-Baladan all the treasures he had was telling (Isa. 39:2). Hezekiah was eager to associate with Babylon, and he tried his hardest to parade his best before the Babylonians so that they would see something worthy in him.

Isaiah's questions reveal how we should be thinking of Hezekiah's actions (Isa. 39:3). You can almost hear the Lord's question to Adam and Eve in the garden echoing in the background, "What is this you have done?" (Gen. 3:13). By asking questions, Isaiah was exposing Babylon for what it was. Certainly a historical nation, Babylon is also symbolic in Scripture for the insatiable desire for human beings to make a name for themselves and live in self-absorption and self-indulgence (Gen. 11:1–9; Rev. 18:2–8). Tragically, the words of death Isaiah prophesied for the nations at the hand of Babylon (39:5–7) didn't bring about the same reaction in Hezekiah that the words of his own death had brought. This time there were no tears, no prayer, and no commitments to the Lord. There was only a self-centered sigh of relief that the exile wouldn't occur during his lifetime (v. 8). What happened to the Hezekiah who committed to passing on the faith to the next generation and to sing in the temple all his remaining days?

These chapters leave us longing for a faithful king, one who is not faithless and fickle but who will fulfill all God's promises. We desire one who will give up the treasures of heaven to come to "Babylon" and save us from exile so that we can live an eternity with peace and security in the New Jerusalem. It is in this Christ that we must place our trust. Why network with the names of this world when we have the Name above all names reigning over us as king, interceding for us as priest, and offering us His words in Scripture as prophet? Let us sing to the Lord today—and every day. Let us pass on the faith to the next generation. And let us go to the house of the Lord weekly to worship God in the midst of His people.

What people of prestige have knocked on your door lately, and how have you been tempted to parade your talents and treasures before them without getting on your knees first and pleading with the Lord to let Him alone be your focus and trust? This passage in Isaiah challenges us to return to faithfulness, rejoicing in the Lord's salvation and remembering His goodness to us so that we can tell the next generation of His love, forgiveness, and faithfulness.

Processing It Together...

1. What do we learn about God in Isaiah 38–39?

2. How does this reshape how we should view our present circumstances?

3. What do we learn about God's Son, Jesus Christ?

4. How should this impact our relationship with God and with others?

5. What do we learn about God's covenant with His people?

6. How are we to live in light of this?

7. How can we apply Isaiah 38–39 to our lives today and in the future?

8. How should we apply this passage in our churches?

9. Look back at "Putting It in Perspective" in your personal study questions. What did you find challenging or encouraging about this lesson?

10. Look back at "Principles and Points of Application." How has this lesson impacted your life?

The Lord Who Comforts

Isaiah 40:1–44:23

Purpose...

Head. What do I need to know from this passage in Scripture?

- The Creator comforts His suffering people whom He has called, giving them counsel and coming as the conquering King, all of which anticipate the person and work of Jesus Christ.

Heart. How does what I learn from this passage affect my internal relationship with the Lord?

- I am a kingdom disciple who is freed from fear by God, my help and my strength.

Hands. How does what I learn from this passage translate into action for God's kingdom?

- I will help those feeling shame understand God's forgiveness.
- I will encourage others to study God's Word.
- I will regularly join with God's people to worship Him.

Personal Study...

Pray. Ask that God will open up your heart and mind as you study His Word. This is His story of redemption that He has revealed to us, and the Holy Spirit is our teacher.

Ponder the Passage. Read Isaiah 40:1–44:23.

- *Point.* What is the point of this passage? How does this relate to the point of the entire book?

- *Persons.* Who are the main people involved in this passage? What characterizes them?

- *Persons of the Trinity.* Where do you see God the Father, God the Son, and God the Holy Spirit in this passage?

- *Puzzling Parts.* Are there any parts of the passage that you don't quite understand or that seem interesting or confusing?

Put It in Perspective.

- *Place in Scripture.* What is the original context of this text? What is the redemptive-historical context—what has or hasn't happened in redemptive history at this point in Scripture? How does this text connect to Christ?

The following questions will help you if you got stuck on any of the previous questions, and they will help you dig a little deeper into the text, putting it all into perspective.

1. **40:1–11.** (a) In light of 39:5–7, how do the opening words of verses 1–2 display God's grace?

   (b) How does Luke use verses 3–4 in the context of Luke 3:1–9?

   (c) What is the point Peter is making when he uses verse 6 in the context of 1 Peter 1:22–25?

   (d) What is the point James is making when he uses verse 8 in the context of James 1:9–11?

(e) What imagery is used in verses 10–11, and how is this ultimately fulfilled (see John 10:11; Heb. 13:20; Rev. 19:11–16)?

2. 40:12–31. (a) What do you learn about God's character in these verses?

(b) How was the Spirit of the Lord active at creation, and how is the Spirit active in the new creation (see Gen. 1:2; John 7:37–39; Acts 2:4; Rev. 22:17)?

(c) What do you learn about the nations?

(d) What do you learn about idolatry?

(e) How does the Lord deal with those who wait for Him?

(f) When Paul uses verse 13 in the context of Romans 11:33–36, what point is he making?

3. 41:1–7. (a) What does verse 1 reveal about the Lord's relationship with the nations?

(b) Later Isaiah will inform us of who this "one" is in verse 2, but for now what is he emphasizing by asking, "Who raised up one from the east?"

(c) How have the coastlands responded to the Lord?

4. 41:8–20. (a) Why did the Lord choose Jacob (see Deut. 7:6–9)?

(b) Note the language of *servant* in verses 8–9. What have you already learned about God's servant in Isaiah (see 20:3; 22:20; 37:35)?

(c) How does the Lord's promise to deliver Israel from all its enemies anticipate Revelation 19:17–21?

(d) How is verse 14 ultimately fulfilled (see Luke 1:68; Gal. 3:13–14)?

(e) How does verse 20 continue the missional theme for God's people, as first seen in Genesis 12:1–3? How is this ultimately fulfilled (see Eph. 2:11–22)?

5. 41:21–29. (a) How does the Lord reveal the futility of idolatry?

(b) Isaiah will soon identify the "one" in verse 25, but for now what do you learn about God regarding this situation?

(c) What do you learn in the New Testament about idolatry (for example, see Col. 3:5; Rev. 9:20)?

6. 42:1–9. (a) What do you learn about "My Servant" here (see 4b above)?

(b) How does Matthew use verse 1 in his gospel (see Matt. 12:15–21)?

(c) How does Jesus bring in the new things?

7. 42:10–17. (a) How are God's people to respond to His conquering might in His salvation and judgment?

(b) How do these verses anticipate Revelation 19:11, 15; 20:15; 21:1–5?

8. 42:18–25. (a) How did Israel respond to the word and works of the Lord?

(b) How do these verses reveal that the ultimate servant cannot be the nation of Israel?

9. 43:1–24. (a) According to verses 1–7, how does God deal with His people in exile, and how does exile end?

(b) How is the truth that salvation is by God alone displayed in verses 8–13?

(c) What does the New Testament say about this (see, for example, Acts 4:12)?

(d) According to verses 14–21, what is the "new thing" God is doing, and how does this anticipate the greater exodus of the Gospels?

(e) How do verses 22–24 confirm Israel's guilt?

(f) If Israel hasn't satisfied God with sacrifices, who has (Heb. 9:11–14)?

10. 43:25–44:5. (a) How does the truth of 43:25 complement Deuteronomy 7:6–9?

(b) Give some examples from Scripture of how Abraham, Isaac, Jacob, and Israel's religious leaders sinned.

(c) How is 44:3 ultimately fulfilled (see Acts 2:1–13)?

11. 44:6–23. (a) What is at least one reason for Israel to trust in God?

(b) Why is it so important to guard one's heart (see also Prov. 4:23; Matt. 12:33–37; 15:18–20)?

(c) What is the basis of Israel's return, and how does this anticipate passages such as 1 John 4:19?

(d) How does verse 23 anticipate Romans 8:18–21?

Principles and Points of Application
12. 40:1–31. (a) How does verse 2 encourage you (think about specific sins you've committed this week)?

(b) How does the truth that God's word will stand forever encourage you to study it consistently?

(c) Who in your life needs to hear that the Lord is a mighty ruler? What about that He is a tender Shepherd? Ask the Lord to give you the opportunity to share this truth with them.

(d) How have you been convicted and challenged to exchange your idols for the Creator?

(e) In what ways are you weary? Memorize verse 31 this week so that it will be a constant comfort for you.

13. **41:1–29.** (a) Have you ever been afraid of the Lord and turned away from Him to the comforts of this world? Describe how the Lord convicted your heart and showed you His love.

(b) What do you fear right now? How do verses 10 and 13 comfort you? Use these verses to personalize a prayer to the Lord: Father, help me not to fear _____, for You are with me; help me to not be dismayed about _____, for You are my God. You will strengthen me and help me regarding _____. You will uphold me with Your righteous right hand as I go through _____. Thank You for holding my hand through _____, and for being the one who helps me through _____.

14. **42:1–25.** (a) Because the Lord has called His children in righteousness and keeps us in His gracious grip, we are to respond by singing praises to His great name. Write out a hymn using what you've learned from this chapter to guide you, and then sing it using one of your favorite hymn tunes.

15. **43:1–24.** (a) How does it comfort you that although the Lord allows even great suffering, it will not consume you?

(b) Memorize verse 4a, and use it this week to encourage a friend doubting God's love.

(c) How could you use these chapters to teach someone who believes all roads lead to heaven that salvation is in Christ alone (see Acts 4:12)?

(d) Search your heart. Are you trying to satisfy God with sacrifices of your own, or are you resting in Christ's final and perfect sacrifice?

16. 43:25–44:23. (a) In what ways has your heart been deluded in the past by the idols of our world? Spend time in prayer, asking the Lord to open your eyes to the lies that your head and heart might be believing.

(b) How often do you remember what the Lord has done for you? Think through all the things He has saved you from and give thanks to Him. Then fix your eyes on eternity and sing of the Lord's words and works as you go about your day.

Putting It All Together...

Suffering is one of the primary means of sanctification God uses in our lives so that we can showcase our Savior instead of ourselves. When another month has passed and the chronic pain is still an unwanted visitor, when the papers stating the terms of divorce lay on the table to be signed, when the teenager slams his door and with it the door of his heart, when your college and career dreams are dashed before your eyes, when the relationship you thought would come hasn't, and when the particular needs of your child or parent drain you to the point of despair, you need the God who created you to comfort and counsel you. Thankfully, He does this with His word, and because of it, we're able to persevere until the Conqueror comes to take us home to glory. We need not fear or look for strength elsewhere. We need not run to appearance and achievements for help. We need not hide behind a facade at church. We need only to behold the face of the One who has become a servant for us so that we might in turn serve Him.

I. The Lord Who Comforts (40:1–41:20)

With the prophecy of the Babylonian exile still ringing in their ears (see Isa. 39:5–7), the people of Judah, who witnessed the Assyrian exile of the Northern Kingdom of Israel in 722 BC, needed to be comforted, especially by the One who was orchestrating history. Judah needed to know for certain that God not only can comfort and redeem but will. Their iniquity would really be pardoned. A voice would cry in the wilderness, which ultimately was John the Baptist, and the glory of the Lord would be revealed, ultimately through Jesus Christ, the Son of God.

Along with being confronted by the truth that the stuff of their storehouses would be carried to Babylon (Isa. 39:6), Judah needed to be reminded that one thing would not move. The word of God stands forever (40:8). In this truth they could put their hope. The same is true for you and me today. The stuff in our storehouses that we think we can't live without is fading, but God's revelation in Scripture is enduring, so that we can pore over it and know Him more, love Him more, trust Him more, and obey Him more.

The mighty ruler of Judah who will conquer the nations is at the same time the tender Shepherd who carries His people home (Isa. 40:9–11). The Creator of the heavens and the earth, the sea and dry land, Israel and the nations does not take counsel with creation (vv. 12–31). Neither should we. If we can create something, it's unworthy of our worship. There is Someone greater who is in control of seas and seeds, people and plans, and we are to lift up our eyes to behold Him. Our ways are before Him, and either we can run to Him in faith and receive His power and strength, or we can run away from Him and come under the wrath of His power and strength.

In this passage, the Lord summons humankind to court. Yet the Judge of all the earth is willing to save people from every tribe, tongue, and nation before He tries them and finds them guilty (Isa. 41:1–7). He is the one who stirs up human deliverers to bring His people out of exile (vv. 2–4). Certainly, then, He is the one who stirs up the final deliverer to bring His people out of sin and the snare of Satan. But humankind often cowers in fear, crafting forms they can worship, engaging in empty exhortations, and telling others to be strong when they've fled from the source of strength (vv. 5–7).

The servant Isaiah, who points forward to a far greater servant, Jesus Christ, speaks the solution (Isa. 41:8–20). The Lord God chose Israel out of His love and on the basis of His covenant, but it would not be Israel that would provide salvation. The Lord God would be with His people through thick and thin, protecting them from the enemies of this world and helping them through history, so that a remnant would emerge even after four hundred years of silence. The hope of redemption that Anna and Simeon were waiting for was rooted in redemptive history (Luke 2:25–38), including Isaiah's prophecies that sing so sweetly of the Lord God opening fountains in valleys and springs of water in dry land (Isa. 41:18).

Such redemption was missional. The Lord God had promised Abraham his descendants would be a blessing to the nations (Gen. 12:1–3). As the nations watched the

Lord raise up a deliverer to lead His people out of Babylon under the leadership of Ezra, Nehemiah, and Zerubbabel, the faithful remnant would see and know the Holy One of Israel had accomplished such salvation. But such a small restoration fell far short of opening rivers on bare heights and making the wilderness a pool of water. It is Christ who comes as the superior servant to turn water into wine and blindness into sight. As those who have been united to Christ, we need only look to Him for comfort in the midst of our crying. His word is the water we need that continually calms us. When we're tempted to find comfort in other things, we must remember those things are powerless to save us, secure us, or strengthen us. The believer who looks to Christ will know the power of His resurrection in her life and will find strength to finish one more school project, encourage her friend in need, change one more diaper, have another late-night talk with her teen, care for her aging parent one more day, or love her husband when he speaks an unkind word. More importantly, she will see and know that only the hand of the gracious Lord enabled her to do it. She beholds "the Father of mercies and God of all comfort, who comforts us in all our tribulation, that we may be able to comfort those who are in any trouble, with the comfort with which we ourselves are comforted by God. For as the sufferings of Christ abound in us, so our consolation also abounds through Christ" (2 Cor. 1:3–5).

II. The Lord Who Conquers (41:21–42:17)

As Isaiah looked ahead to the days of the exile, his attention turned toward God's people living in Babylon and being tempted to worship the idols of that pagan land. Isaiah gave them a strong warning not to do so, a lesson those in his day needed to hear as well. The scene is the courtroom, and the Lord is the King-Judge (Isa. 41:21–29). He invites the nations to parade their gods before Him. But in His invitation, He exposes them for what they really are—good-for-nothings. The Lord would raise up a ruler from the north to deliver His people from idolatrous rulers such as those in Babylon. None of their gods could have seen such a deliverance coming. It is the Lord alone whose works are something worth boasting in and whose image is glorious and trustworthy.

When the Lord made a covenant with His people at Mount Sinai, He forbade them from making a carved image to worship (Ex. 20:4). This is because He already had an image set apart for them to worship. Jesus came as "the brightness of His glory and the express image of His person" (Heb. 1:3). As the apostle John says, "No one has seen God at any time. The only begotten Son, who is in the bosom of the Father, He has declared Him" (John 1:18). Therefore, believers are to turn from trusting in creation to trusting in the Creator. In times of worry, we're to walk with our wonderful counselor. In times of fear, we're to fall to our knees before our Father. In times of distress, we're to dialogue with our deliverer. In times of suffering and sin, we're to seek our Savior. And in times of service, we're to make supplication for the Spirit's blessing on our work so that it's fruitful and effective for the gospel.

After seeing the King, the Lord of hosts, and seeing his own sinfulness, as well as the sinfulness of God's people, Isaiah experienced the forgiveness of God and the call of God to be His servant (Isa. 6:1–8). Isaiah's service would be costly, but not nearly as costly as the service of the servant whom Isaiah's ministry anticipated, Jesus Christ. Israel was also God's servant and was supposed to serve the nations by serving the Lord. In this way the Gentile nations would see how great Israel's God is and worship Him. But Israel failed in this task, revealing the need for a greater servant. In each servant passage in the book of Isaiah, then, we are pointed forward to a single figure who would ultimately be revealed in the New Testament as Jesus Christ.

In the context of Isaiah, these verses (42:1–9) serve to strengthen the Babylonian exiles as they wonder if there's any hope for justice to be established on the earth. The Creator and covenant Lord shouts a resounding yes into their despair. The God who gives breath to Israel's enemies, as well as to Israel, has not forgotten He has called them. Since He cannot be unfaithful to His promises, He will raise up His servant to be a light for the nations and a liberator for the needy. He will do it in His own way and in His own time in order to receive the greatest glory. He is bringing to pass His new covenant promises in the light of the world. Therefore, the exiles can sing a new song because there is coming a new day (vv. 10–17). But it is not just a new day for Israel. God's people will come forth from all nations to give glory to the Lord. The King of all the earth, the mighty ruler of the nations, will be victorious over all. His peace and restraint will give way to war and revenge so that He can lead and guide His people on level ground and put the idolaters to shame. Behold, He will make all things new (Rev. 21:5).

Jesus came as the light of the world and the covenant keeper to open blind eyes and liberate the oppressed. He came full of grace and truth in order to inaugurate God's kingdom in peace and restraint. But there's coming a day when He will come on a war-horse in order to judge those who call metal images gods and forsake the one living and true God. Today is the day of salvation. Let us exchange the idols we hold so dearly in our hearts for the one living and true God, so that we might give glory to Him alone.

III. The Lord Who Creates (42:18–43:21)

The Creator of His people's ears and eyes calls them to account for their deafness and blindness in light of all His works and words (Isa. 42:18–25). What should have been a glorious existence—God's people living in God's place with God's presence underneath God's rule—had become a heated one. But even the heat did not melt their hearts. Their spiritual blindness and deafness prevailed.

But the Creator is also the Redeemer, and this is precisely Israel's hope (43:1–21). Because He has called Israel by name, some from Israel (the remnant) would call Him by name. Though they would experience fiery trials, they would not be consumed because the Lord is the Savior of His people. Because of His great love, He remains "God with us" even when His people are far from Him. The Creator would not leave His people in exile but would restore them to their land from all the nations to which they'd been scattered. Like the exodus out of Egypt, the Lord would do a new thing and bring His people out of Babylon. He alone is the Lord God, Creator and Redeemer, King and Holy One. What looked impossible would become historical fact before their eyes, and the purpose of redemption was the same as that of the exodus from Egypt—that His people might declare His praise.

Jesus was not blind; rather, He came to make the blind man see. He became to us righteousness from God so that He might fulfill the law and make it glorious. He came to rescue and restore those in the prison house of sin. He created all things and accomplished redemption. When we walk through fiery trials, Christ is with us, keeping us from being consumed. We need not fear because Jesus is Immanuel, God with us. He saves all those who have been chosen by the Father, giving the drink of eternal life, so that they might declare His praise. With such truth ringing in our ears, we should take courage, calling others to look to Him for salvation. There is no other name by which humankind can be saved. And when our sister is in the stormy waters or the flaming fire, we can remind her of the Lord her God, the Holy One of Israel, her Savior. She need not fear for her children's safety, or her husband's health, or the success of her career, or her adult child's marriage. He offers her the drink of life that will refresh her soul so that she might declare His praise even in the darkness.

IV. The Lord Who Calls (43:22–44:23)

Israel did not call on the Lord who called them first as His people (Isa. 43:22–24). Their sacrifices did not satisfy their Savior. Instead, they burdened the Lord with their sin. Yet for His own sake He would blot out their transgression (v. 25). With the rich history of disobedience, beginning with Adam and stretching to Noah, Abraham, Moses, and David, not to mention the rebellion of the leaders and the people throughout this history, it's amazing grace that the Lord continued to call His people to return to Him (vv. 26–28).

The Lord would pour out His Spirit on His people so that they could call on the name of the Lord (Isa. 44:1–5). Apart from the Spirit unstopping dear ears and making blind eyes see, nobody would respond to the Lord's call. But the only God, the rock of salvation, exposes the inconsistency and irrationality of idolatry so that His people might turn to Him, the Redeemer (vv. 6–20). Such redemption will call forth not just praise from His people but from all creation (vv. 21–23).

The Spirit of life has set those who are in Christ free from sin and death. By sending His own Son, the Father condemned sin in Jesus's flesh so that Christ's righteousness would be imputed to us. We are to walk according to the Spirit, exemplifying life and peace. On this side of glory, we groan with creation to be set free from the sufferings of this life. And we groan with hope because God has promised not just redemption but also the consummation of His kingdom. There is coming a day when we will obtain the freedom of the glory God has for us as His children, and creation along with us. The

Spirit within us is the security we have to hope for such glory. He is the down payment, the firstfruits, the one who is making all things new, even now as He slowly transforms us into Christlikeness, until we reach perfection in glory.

In your suffering, what do you fear, and where are you turning for help? This lesson exhorts us not to turn to the gods of this world. The ice cream won't ultimately soothe, we can't run enough miles to escape, the new outfit can't take away the pain, social media will leave us feeling emptier than when we started to scroll, and entertainment fades into the background. There is only one place to turn when we are tempted to sing the same old song of sin and misery. The gracious God holds our hand, strengthens our step, delivers us from darkness, and sings over us a new song. Therefore, let us sing a new song to Him, knowing that our suffering accomplishes the sovereign purposes of God.

Processing It Together...

1. What do we learn about God in Isaiah 40:1–44:23?

2. How does this reshape how we should view our present circumstances?

3. What do we learn about God's Son, Jesus Christ?

4. How should this impact our relationship with God and with others?

5. What do we learn about God's covenant with His people?

6. How are we to live in light of this?

7. How can we apply Isaiah 40:1–44:23 to our lives today and in the future?

8. How should we apply this passage in our churches?

9. Look back at "Putting It in Perspective" in your personal study questions. What did you find challenging or encouraging about this lesson?

10. Look back at "Principles and Points of Application." How has this lesson impacted your life?

The Superior Servant

Isaiah 44:24–55:13

Purpose...

Head. What do I need to know from this passage in Scripture?

- Even more startling than the fact that God raised up Cyrus to deliver His people from the Babylonian exile is the fact that He raised up the Suffering Servant to ultimately deliver His people from the exile of sin and death.

Heart. How does what I learn from this passage affect my internal relationship with the Lord?

- I am a kingdom disciple who has come to Christ and can truly know joy and peace in Him.

Hands. How does what I learn from this passage translate into action for God's kingdom?

- I will boldly speak truth to those around me.
- I will help others see the danger of worldliness and pray for those in rebellion against the Lord.
- I will show compassion to the hurting and help them suffer in a way that glorifies God.
- I will teach the truths of the faith to the next generation and help them apply it to their lives.

Personal Study...

Pray. Ask that God will open up your heart and mind as you study His Word. This is His story of redemption that He has revealed to us, and the Holy Spirit is our teacher.

Ponder the Passage. Read Isaiah 44:24–55:13. I recommend dividing this week's study into the following: day 1 (44:24–46:13); day 2 (47:1–48:22); day 3 (49:1–50:11); day 4 (51:1–52:12); day 5 (52:13–55:13).

- *Point.* What is the point of this passage? How does this relate to the point of the entire book?

- *Persons.* Who are the main people involved in this passage? What characterizes them?

- *Persons of the Trinity.* Where do you see God the Father, God the Son, and God the Holy Spirit in this passage?

- *Puzzling Parts.* Are there any parts of the passage that you don't quite understand or that seem interesting or confusing?

Put It in Perspective.

- *Place in Scripture.* What is the original context of this text? What is the redemptive-historical context—what has or hasn't happened in redemptive history at this point in Scripture? How does this text connect to Christ?

The following questions will help you if you got stuck on any of the previous questions, and they will help you dig a little deeper into the text, putting it all into perspective.

1. 44:24–45:8. (a) How do 44:28 and 45:1 relate to 41:2, 25 and 43:14–15?

(b) Does Cyrus know the Lord, and why is this significant in terms of what kind of deliverer Israel was looking for?

(c) In light of these verses, how does Cyrus anticipate Christ (see, for example, John 10:11; Heb. 13:20; 1 Peter 5:4)?

2. 45:9–13. (a) How does verse 11 recall Exodus 4:22?

(b) What work will Cyrus do for the Lord, and why is it significant that he won't be paid or rewarded?

(c) How does Jesus fulfill the covenant name of the Lord (see Ex. 3:14–15; John 6:35; 8:12; 10:7; 11:25; 14:6; 15:1)?

3. 45:14–25. (a) Despite Israel's rebellion, how will they be a light to the nations?

(b) How do verses 20–22 reflect Genesis 12:1–3; 22:18?

(c) How does verse 23 anticipate Philippians 2:9–11?

(d) How does verse 25 anticipate Romans 5:15–17?

4. 46:1–13. (a) Use a study Bible or other resource to learn about the Babylonian gods Bel and Nebo. What did you learn about them, and why would Isaiah use them in his argument?

(b) Why would Israel have had a hard time with a pagan deliverer? What reasons does the Lord give them to trust Him?

(c) How are the outlines of this chapter and Romans 1:18–25 to 3:21–22 to 5:17 similar?

5. 47:1–48:22. (a) How does chapter 47 bring the argument regarding the futility of idolatry to a climax?

(b) How does Babylon's downfall here look back to Genesis 11:1–9 and toward Revelation 18?

(c) How does chapter 48 bring Israel's sin to a climax? Note specifically verses 1, 4–8, 18, 22.

(d) How does 48:3 look back to chapter 47?

(e) How does 48:6 look back to 42:1–9 and forward to 49:1–13; 50:4–9; 52:13–53:12?

(f) How does 48:10–11, 21 recall the exodus theme (see Ex. 3:18; 17:1–7; Deut. 4:20), and 48:19 the Abrahamic covenant (Gen. 15:5; 22:17)?

6. 49:1–6. (a) How far does the servant's ministry reach?

(b) How do you know from verses 5–6 that "My servant, O Israel" in verse 3 cannot refer to national Israel?

(c) Who is the Servant (compare verse 2 with Revelation 1:16–18)?

(d) How does Luke use verse 6 in Acts 13:44–47?

7. 49:7–13. (a) How would these verses have comforted Judah, who had heard of the exile of the Northern Kingdom in 722 BC and were now hearing about the coming Babylonian exile for them?

(b) How does Paul use verse 8 in the context of 2 Corinthians 5:20–6:2?

(c) How does John use verse 10 in the context of Revelation 7:13–17?

8. 49:14–50:11. (a) Zion was another name for Jerusalem, which symbolized God's presence, promises, and protection, but because of Israel's rebellion it had become desolate during the exile. In verse 14 Zion is personified as rebellious Israel. What does Zion charge God with, and how does God answer it in 49:15–17 and 50:1–3?

(b) What do verses 15–16 have in common with Jesus's lament over Jerusalem in Luke 13:34–35?

(c) How do verses 22–26 reflect Exodus 19:4–6; Deuteronomy 9:4–6; and Revelation 16:5–6?

(d) How is the word of God prominent in the Servant's ministry? How do you see this in Christ's ministry (give specific examples)?

(e) How does Christ fulfill the description of the Servant in 50:4–9 (see Matt. 11:28; John 14:31; Luke 22:63–65; Rom. 8:33–34; 1 Tim. 3:16)?

(f) Contrast the response of the righteous and the response of the rebellious in 50:10–11.

9. **51:1–52:12.** (a) What encouragement could the exiles draw from God's work in the past with Abraham and Sarah (see Gen. 17:15–21; 21:1–3)?

(b) What is emphasized in a similar refrain in 51:6, 8?

(c) In 51:10–11, how does Isaiah use the exodus from Egypt to describe what the Lord is doing?

(d) According to 51:16, what is the motivation for the Lord's action in 51:21–22?

(e) How does Paul use 52:5 in the context of Romans 2:17–24? How does he use 52:7 in the context of Romans 10:12–17? How does he use 52:11 in the context of 2 Corinthians 6:14–7:1?

(f) In what way does 52:12 reflect exodus language (see Ex. 12:11; 14:19–20)?

10. **52:13–53:12.** How do the following passages use this Servant Song?

John 12:37–38

Acts 8:27–35

Romans 10:14–17

Romans 15:20–21

1 Peter 2:21–25

11. 54:1–55:13. (a) How does the covenant faithfulness of the Lord come to the fore in chapter 54? How would this have encouraged the Judah of Isaiah's day, which was looking toward the future Babylonian exile, as well as the exiles who would hear these words in the future?

(b) How does Paul use 54:1 in the context of Galatians 4:21–31, and how does Jesus use 54:13 in the context of John 6:43–51?

(c) How does God's purpose for Abraham to be a blessing to the nations (Gen. 12:3) become prominent in chapter 55?

(d) What are the major themes of chapter 55, and how are they seen in the New Testament (see, for example, Matt. 11:28; John 6:27; 7:37–39; Acts 3:13; 5:31; 13:34; 2 Cor. 9:10; Rev. 17:14; 19:16)?

Principles and Points of Application
12. 44:24–45:25. (a) How is the Lord using the unexpected to bring you blessing, and how are you responding to it? How does it comfort you that Jesus, the Great Shepherd and ruler of the nations, is your prophet, priest, and king?

(b) How could you use 45:22 to help a friend understand the message of Isaiah— indeed, of the whole Bible—and how does this verse motivate you to engage in missions?

13. **46:1–13.** What idols or addictions are you carrying in order to find security instead of trusting in the Lord who carries you? What does verse 12 say about the hearts of people who worship idols, and does this convict you?

14. **47:1–48:22.** (a) How could you use chapter 47 to help a youth or a friend see the danger and futility of worldliness?

(b) The description of stubborn Israel in chapter 48 is a picture of all our hearts apart from God's grace. How do these verses help you appreciate the Lord's graciousness and faithfulness?

(c) Spend time in prayer for those you know who are rebelling against the Lord. Consider sending them a note of encouragement, letting them know you've prayed for them.

15. **49:1–13.** (a) As believers united to Christ, the light for the nations, we too are a light for the nations and have the privilege of sending missionaries, praying for them, or going ourselves to proclaim the good news to the other side of our towns, our countries, or the world. In what ways are you actively participating in this?

(b) In what ways has the Lord comforted you and shown you compassion this week? Think of someone you know who needs you to show the comfort and compassion of the Lord, and how can you do that this week?

16. **49:14–50:11.** (a) How does it encourage you that the Lord has engraved you on the palms of His hand? How could you use this truth to encourage a child?

(b) How is Christ sustaining you in your weariness through His word? Who do you need to share Scripture with this week to remind them of Christ's sustaining power?

(c) What darkness are you walking in? Write out a prayer for trust and reliance on the Lord. Then memorize 50:10.

17. **51:1–52:12.** (a) Our motivation for teaching the next generation the truths of the Lord should come from the understanding that the Lord's salvation is to all generations. How are you investing in the next generation, teaching them the truths of the faith and helping them apply it to their lives?

(b) Which child, friend, or neighbor of yours needs to hear the truth that God pleads the cause of His people? Make every effort to tell them this week.

18. **52:13–55:13.** (a) Since Christ suffered, we know that we too will suffer. Yet our suffering is not in vain. The testing of our faith, if proved genuine, will result in praise, honor, and glory at Christ's return (1 Peter 1:7). How can you endure your present suffering in a way that glorifies God?

(b) How could you use 54:4–8 to encourage a woman suffering in a difficult marriage or a woman who has endured divorce or widowhood? How do these verses encourage you?

(c) The Lord graciously calls "Come to Me" (55:3). Whether it's for the first or the hundredth time, we need to continually come to Christ. We don't hear the gospel once and then run the Christian life on its fumes. We must return to gospel truth each moment of each day. Who do you need to remind of the gospel today—a child who is trying to do life on her own, a friend who is lonely, a coworker suffering physically, or a neighbor who feels stressed with her schedule?

Putting It All Together...

Every day we are bombarded by marketers with the message, "Come, buy and eat!" Whether it's the realtor selling property in the mountains; or the trip advisor planning your cruise; or the local restaurant inviting you to try their new dish; or, more sobering, the pornographic website beckoning you to come feast your eyes on inappropriate images, we daily have the opportunity to find our joy and peace in the temporal instead of the eternal. These chapters in Isaiah provide another and better invitation. The Lord cries, "Come to Me!"

I. God's Shepherd, Cyrus (44:24–48:22)

Isaiah has already alerted us that the Lord will raise up someone from the north and the east to deliver His people (41:2, 25), but now the deliverer is named. Think of the shock when God's people, who were expecting a Davidic deliverer, heard that the Lord was going to deliver them by the hands of a Gentile king. Yet the Creator of all and Redeemer of His people was doing just that. Cyrus would free God's people from exile in Babylon, and Jerusalem would be inhabited again (44:28). The Lord even uses those who don't bow their knee to Him to accomplish His redemptive purposes and reveal that He alone is Lord.

In this created world, salvation and redemption bear fruit because the Redeemer is orchestrating all things for His glory (Isa. 45:8). The exiles need not fear anyone or anything other than the Lord. The One who sets His exiles free at the hand of a foreign king with no reward is the only one worthy of reward (v. 13).

As the nations see the Creator take the hand of His created and lead them back to the land of promise, they will know Israel's God is the one living and true God (Isa. 45:14). Those who worshiped idols will be put to shame because their gods can't stand in the face of the true God (vv. 15–17). Righteousness and salvation are found in only one source, and it's to Him that every knee will one day bow (vv. 21–23). Justification and glory are found in the Lord alone (v. 25).

Jesus declared, "I am the good shepherd" (John 10:11). He came to lead God's people out of sin and darkness to righteousness and light. He is the Anointed One, the Messiah, King of kings, High Priest of all priests. He is the ruler of the nations, and in Him alone is salvation found. Through His atoning sacrifice He sets God's people free to live for Him. In Him the offer of eternal life stands firm and steadfast. Today is the day of salvation, and every tongue is invited to turn to Him and pledge allegiance to His great name, the only name by which we can be justified and glorified. All those who know this anointed Shepherd have been commissioned to turn to the ends of the earth and declare His praise so that the nations might turn to Him and be saved.

Isaiah exposes Babylon's gods for what they are—burdens that beasts carry into exile (Isa. 46:1–2). The gods who were supposed to carry the people into the future were helpless before the true God, who truly carries His people in the past, present, and future (vv. 3–4). The Creator cannot be compared with His creation (v. 5). Yet His people remained stubborn in heart, refusing righteousness (v. 12). Amazingly, for His glory the Lord would put salvation in Zion (v. 13; see also Heb. 12:22–24).

Babylon's end was sealed from the beginning (Isa. 47:1–15). The old cry from the Tower of Babel continued throughout the history of humankind: "We want to be God!" (Gen. 11:1–9). Those who make their own thrones lose them (Isa. 47:1). Lovers of pleasure who find their security in something other than the Lord will fall (vv. 8–9). What is done in the darkness is seen by the light and is ultimately revealed by it (vv. 10–11). Stargazing may bring peace to the soul for a moment, but in the end, it doesn't save you (vv. 12–13). Those who reject the only Savior are in the end consumed by God's fire (vv. 14–15).

Chapter 47 brings the argument regarding the futility of idolatry to a climax. It is a chilling picture of what will happen to the worldliness around us and those who bow to it on the final day of judgment. Our God is a consuming fire (Heb. 12:29). If we don't run to Him in faith, we will run away from Him in fear and terror we've never known before on the day He returns on a war-horse (Rev. 19:11–16). Sadly, even in the church, many have made Jesus out to be anyone but the Judge of all the earth.

Israel needed to hear that God is a consuming fire. In chapter 48 we reach the climax of just how bad God's chosen people had become. They confessed the God of Israel, but not in truth (v. 1). They had become obstinate and ascribed the words and works of God to their carved images (vv. 4–5). They were rebels from birth, dealing treacherously with truth (v. 8). Because God cannot give His glory to another, He has to save His chosen people (vv. 9–11). Though only a remnant will be saved, the Lord, for His own sake, will do it (vv. 12–17). The salvation of God's people is not a possibility, but a certainty. The Creator and Redeemer will lead His people out of exile. Though they had forsaken the covenant blessings that could have been theirs (vv. 18–19), they would go out from Babylon and return home. Just as in the exodus of old, when the Lord delivered His people with a mighty arm from the furnace of Egypt and led them through the wilderness, providing water from the rock, He would again lead His people out of Babylon so that they could serve Him (vv. 20–22).

Chapter 48 is a picture of us all apart from Christ. Even while we were hostile to God, Christ reconciled us to the Father (Rom. 5:10). We too are rebels from birth, rejecting truth and embracing error. It is only the grace of God that has saved us. Therefore, as we look at our family members and our friends and neighbors who continue to rebel, our hope is not in them changing but in the Lord who can change the person. He can take the wickedest heart and make waters of living water pour forth by the power of His Spirit.

II. God's Superior Servant, Christ (49:1–55:13)
We've seen the heinousness of Israel's sin, and we've gotten a glimpse of the Servant in 42:1–9. Now the second Servant Song (49:1–13) continues to answer the question

that is looming large: What hope does Israel have if there is no peace for the wicked? This Servant Song clarifies for us that the Servant is not Israel because the Servant will bring Israel back to God. This Servant will be given worldwide recognition. He will be a prophet, but more than a prophet, because in Him God will display His beauty. His message will fall on deaf ears in Israel, yet the Lord will vindicate Him. He is a light for the nations, bringing salvation to the ends of the earth. He will be given as a covenant to God's people, guiding peoples from every nation by springs of water and displaying God's comfort and compassion to all creation.

All the covenant promises of God are yes in Christ (2 Cor. 1:20). Christ offered comfort and displayed compassion to those who received Him but received suffering from those who rejected Him. He is the light of the world, and whoever follows Him will have the light of life (John 8:12). He told the Samaritan woman at the well that whoever drinks the water He gives will never thirst again (John 4:14). And before He ascended to heaven, He commissioned His disciples to be His lights (witnesses) to the end of the earth (Acts 1:8; see also 13:47).

God's discouraged people, personified as Zion (49:14), question His love. The city of Zion (Jerusalem), which was a symbol of God's presence, protection, and promises, was in ruins (v. 19), so they charged God with forsaking and forgetting them. But Isaiah affirms that just as a mother can't forget her child, the Lord cannot forget them (v. 15). Even in exile, where shame seems to steal Zion's strength, the Lord will prove that He is the one who removes their shame (vv. 22–23).

In 50:1–3 the Lord again answers the charge brought against Him in 49:14 that He had forsaken and forgotten His people. He lays the blame at Israel's feet. The Lord had called, but no one had answered. They had rejected the Creator and Redeemer. How foolish! There is no other person who can take away our transgressions or erase our iniquities. Judgment awaits all who refuse the call of the Lord.

You may feel as if the Lord has forgotten you, but He has engraved you on the palms of His hand. Your Redeemer and Savior will not fail to display His redemptive power in your life, regardless of how dark it may seem. The same God who dried up the sea so the people could walk on dry ground to escape from Egypt and who restored the Babylonian exiles has given His only Son, Jesus Christ, to redeem us from exile in sin to salvation in Him. We are the Father's children because Christ has accomplished our redemption, and the Spirit applies it to our lives. We need not hang our heads in shame. We must look up and behold our God!

The third Servant Song (50:4–9) reveals that the Servant who will save Israel will suffer greatly. But the suffering will not deter Him from accomplishing His purpose because He is confident He won't ultimately be put to shame but will be vindicated. When Paul writes to Timothy about the greatness of the mystery of godliness, He says that Christ

was manifested in the flesh,
Justified in the Spirit,

Seen by angels,
Preached among the Gentiles,
Believed on in the world,
Received up in glory. (1 Tim. 3:16)

This is the Servant with whom believers are united. Therefore, no one can contend with us. The love of our heavenly Father is certain because Christ has secured our salvation (Rom. 8:31–39).

Because of the Servant's work, God's people are to trust in Him and rely on His light to lead them through whatever darkness they encounter in exile (Isa. 49:10–11). All those seeking the Lord have only to remember how He worked through Abraham and Sarah's lives, bringing forth the promised child and preserving the godly line (51:2). *Gladness*—not *sadness*—would be the final word (v. 3). The Lord's righteousness would reign supreme (vv. 4–8). The same Lord who delivered His people from Egypt remains committed to comforting, saving, and establishing His people (vv. 9–16). Their salvation is not at the mercy of an unjust judge but of the righteous Judge who pleads the cause of His people, taking the cup of wrath from them and putting it in the hands of their enemies instead (vv. 17–23).

When we reach the Gospels, we see the greatest of Abraham's sons, Jesus Christ. He is the one who pleads the cause of God's people. Although Jesus pled with His Father to take the cup of wrath away if He was willing, He was committed to drink it so that you and I would be saved (Luke 22:42). He ever lives to plead the cause of God's people, as our Mediator and High Priest who has made the final and atoning sacrifice and who presently intercedes for us at the Father's righteous right hand. On judgment day, all God's enemies will have to drink the cup of wrath. Only those who are united to Christ in faith will be spared because the Savior drank it for us. This should motivate us to proclaim the gospel to our friend who thinks all roads lead to heaven, or our neighbor who doesn't believe in religion, or our family member who is too busy with her career to think of Christ. Such proclamation begins with prayer, pleading with the Lord for their salvation. The feet of those who bring the gospel message are beautiful indeed (Isa. 52:7; Rom. 10:15).

The Lord makes it clear that exile is not the final word (Isa. 52:1–12). He will redeem His people with His holy arm for the entire world to see (v. 10). The final Servant Song (52:13–53:12) climactically shows how He will do it. The Servant will be wise and exalted, but before a picture can form in our minds of a handsome king dressed in royal robes, we learn that His appearance will be so disfigured that it will be astonishing. The root of Jesse had no beauty according to the world's eyes. Despised and rejected by humankind, He knew pain well. Yet He came to carry the sins of God's people; through His stripes we are healed. The Shepherd sacrificed His life for God's sheep. Oppression and affliction didn't open His mouth. Silently submissive, He died with the wicked for the wicked ones God was saving. It was the Lord's will to crush Him that He might be the offering for guilt and through His death bring life to many.

Six of the verses from this fourth and final Servant Song are cited in the New Testament, declaring Christ as the Suffering Servant. Peter knew this section of Isaiah well:

"[He] committed no sin,
Nor was deceit found in His mouth";
who, when He was reviled, did not revile in return; when He suffered, He did not threaten, but committed Himself to Him who judges righteously; who Himself bore our sins in His own body on the tree, that we, having died to sins, might live for righteousness—by whose stripes you were healed. For you were like sheep going astray, but have now returned to the Shepherd and Overseer of your souls. (1 Peter 2:22–25)

As believers, we are called to follow in His footsteps as we suffer in this world. Because He has lived a life of perfect righteousness for us and died an atoning death on our behalf, we are to say no to sin and yes to holiness.

With the four Servant Songs complete, all of which reveal how God is going to save Israel, Isaiah breaks into the comforting news of chapter 54. Although Israel failed to be a light to the nations and bear sons of Abraham who feared the Lord, they could sing because of the Servant. Exile was grim, but enlarged tents were coming—their family, the church of God, was going to grow! They won't remember the shame of exile during which they felt like an abandoned wife but instead will know the passionate love of their husband, the God of the whole earth (v. 5). The desertion of exile gives way to delight in the everlasting love of the Lord. The flood of God's anger that swept over them in Babylon gives way to peace and righteousness. Just as the Servant will be vindicated before a watching world, so will the servants of the Servant.

When the Jews grumbled about Jesus's claim that He was the bread that came down from heaven, He used this passage from Isaiah to declare that He was the fulfillment of the truth that all God's children will be taught by the Lord (Isa. 54:13; John 6:45). What will you do with this Jesus, dear reader? As we submit ourselves to Scripture, the Spirit of Christ illuminates our hearts and minds and transforms us. Those who grumble against Him (and His people) will not succeed; the servants of the Lord can remain steadfast in the truth that our heritage is with the Lord.

Chapter 55 makes no sense without the Servant Songs that have preceded it. How can we be invited to come to the Lord and buy luxurious food without price? This chapter throws wide open the gates of salvation, offering it to the entire world, whoever will come. As the chapter unfolds, we learn that the Lord is inviting us to "come to Me" (v. 3), so that we might live on the basis of the covenant of grace secured by the Davidic king, Jesus Christ. It is through the Servant's work that salvation comes to the nations. But the day of salvation has a limit. The compassion of the Lord calls today, but the day of judgment is coming. The gospel message goes forth today, sowing seed in the hearts of many people. God's salvific purposes will be accomplished. Many people will sing of joy and peace. God's people will never be completely cut off. Glory is ahead; creation will be liberated, and God's people will know fullness of joy in the presence of their King.

❖ ❖ ❖ ❖

In a world that is calling out in numerous different ways, "Come, buy and eat!" our Lord and Savior Jesus Christ cries, "Come to Me, all you who labor and are heavy laden, and I will give you rest" (Matt. 11:28). He is the bread of heaven that satisfies. His words breathe life to our weary souls. He has accomplished our salvation; He is accomplishing our sanctification and will one day perfect it in glorification.

In light of His grace, let us call on the Lord of compassion who abundantly pardons our sins. His ways are better than ours, His thoughts greater. Let us exchange empty words for the words of truth that will always bear fruit, and let us give up seeking satisfaction in anyone other than Christ so that we might know true peace and joy.

Processing It Together...

1. What do we learn about God in Isaiah 44:24–55:13?

2. How does this reshape how we should view our present circumstances?

3. What do we learn about God's Son, Jesus Christ?

4. How should this impact our relationship with God and with others?

5. What do we learn about God's covenant with His people?

6. How are we to live in light of this?

7. How can we apply Isaiah 44:24–55:13 to our lives today and in the future?

8. How should we apply this passage in our churches?

9. Look back at "Putting It in Perspective" in your personal study questions. What did you find challenging or encouraging about this lesson?

10. Look back at "Principles and Points of Application." How has this lesson impacted your life?

The Lord Sanctifies His People

Isaiah 56:1–59:13

Purpose...

Head. What do I need to know from this passage in Scripture?

- The Lord does not just save and shepherd His people; He also sanctifies them.

Heart. How does what I learn from this passage affect my internal relationship with the Lord?

- I am a kingdom disciple who has been given everything I need by God's power to live a life of holiness.

Hands. How does what I learn from this passage translate into action for God's kingdom?

- I will pray for the conversion of people from every nation and proclaim the gospel boldly.
- I will set aside Sunday as a day of corporate worship.
- I will dwell with others in understanding, selflessness, self-control, and humility.

Personal Study...

Pray. Ask that God will open up your heart and mind as you study His Word. This is His story of redemption that He has revealed to us, and the Holy Spirit is our teacher.

Ponder the Passage. Read Isaiah 56:1–59:13.

- *Point.* What is the point of this passage? How does this relate to the point of the entire book?

- *Persons.* Who are the main people involved in this passage? What characterizes them?

- *Persons of the Trinity.* Where do you see God the Father, God the Son, and God the Holy Spirit in this passage?

- *Puzzling Parts.* Are there any parts of the passage that you don't quite understand or that seem interesting or confusing?

Put It in Perspective.

- *Place in Scripture.* What is the original context of this text? What is the redemptive-historical context—what has or hasn't happened in redemptive history at this point in Scripture? How does this text connect to Christ?

The following questions will help you if you got stuck on any of the previous questions, and they will help you dig a little deeper into the text, putting it all into perspective.

1. **56:1–8.** (a) How do we know from the broader context of Isaiah that verse 1 is not teaching works righteousness? What is it addressing?

(b) What do you learn about the Sabbath from Exodus 16:22–29; 20:8–11; 31:12–17; Matthew 12:8; Hebrews 4:9?

(c) How do these verses fulfill what is written in 49:5 and 55:1, as well as in Genesis 12:3 and 1 Kings 8:41–43?

(d) How does Jesus use verse 7 during His earthly ministry (see Luke 19:45–46)?

(e) How is verse 8 reflected in Jesus's words in John 10:14–16?

2. 56:9–12. (a) What were Israel's leaders supposed to be like (see 1 Kings 9:4–5; Ps. 78:70–72)?

(b) How is Christ the perfect Shepherd of God's people (see John 10:11, 14–18; Heb. 13:20; 1 Peter 5:4; Rev. 7:17)?

3. 57:1–21. (a) What kind of memorial was Israel supposed to set up behind their door and doorpost (see Deut. 6:4–9)?

(b) What is the distinction in these verses between God's rebellious people whom He has chosen to save and the wicked?

(c) How do these verses anticipate Luke 1:49–55; Ephesians 2:14–17; Hebrews 13:15; and Revelation 19:1–4?

4. 58:1–14. (a) How does this chapter relate to Isaiah 1:10–20?

(b) Why is keeping the Sabbath a good indication of where one's heart is?

(c) How does verse 7 anticipate Jesus's words in Matthew 12:1–8 and 25:34–40?

5. 59:1–13. (a) Where do these verses lay the blame for the breach of covenant? Why?

(b) How does verse 2 anticipate John 3:19–20; 12:35; 1 John 1:6?

(c) How does Paul use verse 7 in the context of Romans 3:9–18 and verse 20 in Romans 11:25–27?

Principles and Points of Application

6. **56:1–8.** (a) How do these verses motivate you toward evangelism and missions?

(b) In what ways does your church encourage you to keep the Lord's Day holy? How do you, or you and your family, seek to make Sunday different from the other days of the week?

7. **56:9–12.** Spend time in prayer asking the Lord to make you into a godly shepherdess who leads those under your care (whether it's children, other women, or workers you manage) with understanding, selflessness, self-control, and humility.

8. **57:1–21.** (a) Given the increasing hostility toward Christianity in our country and in the world, how does verse 2 encourage you? How do you see evidence of Christian influence decreasing in your school district, city, and neighborhood, and how are you responding?

(b) How have you set up your "memorial" to the Lord in your home?

(c) In what ways have you been guilty of crying out to your collection of idols (think about comfort, control, convenience, career advancement, popularity, power, and possessions)?

(d) Spend time in thanksgiving for what the Lord has done for you through Christ, and then offer up a sacrifice of praise to God—the fruit of lips recognizing His great name (Heb. 13:15).

(e) Spend time in prayer for the unbelievers you know, asking the Lord to save them from wickedness.

9. **58:1–14.** (a) How have you been guilty of hypocrisy and ritualism (just going through the motions with your heart far from God) in your relationship with Christ?

(b) Memorize James 1:27. Then implement its truth.

(c) In what ways are you tempted to do your own thing on Sundays instead of honor the Lord's Day?

10. **59:1–13.** (a) In what ways have you experienced hindered fellowship with the Lord when you are not dwelling in unity with others? How does it affect your Bible reading and prayer life?

(b) What should your heart attitude be as you await the consummation of Christ's kingdom (Rom. 8:23)?

Putting It All Together...

Have you ever known a hypocrite—someone who says to do one thing but does another? If we're honest, we all know a hypocrite. The correct answer to that question first and foremost is, "Yes, I know myself." How often have we told our children not to get angry at one another because anger does not bring about the righteousness of God, yet we get angry with them? How often do we judge our husband for not doing duties we think he should do, holding him up to our own standard instead of to God's Word? How often have we told a friend not to worry about her relationships when we lay awake worrying about ours? How often have we been sweet at women's Bible study but selfish at home? We are masters at preaching what we don't practice.

These chapters in Isaiah are a warning to us. The Lord is not interested in our show; He is interested in our salvation and sanctification, which He alone can and will accomplish in the lives of His daughters.

I. The Lord Sanctifies His People (56:1–8)

In the previous chapter the Lord opened wide the invitation to His feast:

> Ho! Everyone who thirsts,
> Come to the waters;
> And you who have no money,
> Come, buy and eat.
> Yes, come, buy wine and milk
> Without money and without price. (55:1)

Indeed, the Lord's salvation is free for His children. But once a person is saved, how should she then live? That question is what this lesson addresses. The people of God are to look different because of His salvation. God's people are to keep justice and do righteousness.

In these final chapters of his book (56–66), Isaiah will broaden his focus to include the eschatological day of the Lord, which will include salvation for God's people and judgment for the wicked. One of the greatest tests that reveal a person's faith or lack thereof is what they do with their days. So Isaiah speaks about the Sabbath. Keeping the Sabbath is the fourth of the Ten Commandments the Lord God gave Moses on Mount Sinai (Ex. 20:8–11; Deut. 5:12–15). It was also the sign that the Lord gave to Israel so that they would know the Lord is the one who sanctifies His people. It was a sign that the Lord created the heaven and earth in six days and rested on the seventh (Ex. 31:13). His people were to find rest and refreshment on this day too.

Isaiah 55 reminded us that God's plan from the beginning has been to call a people to Himself from every nation. Here we learn that foreigners and eunuchs are also given the right to be sons and daughters of God. It is not physical Israel, but spiritual Israel (the person who loves the name of the Lord and serves Him faithfully) who is saved. The Lord will bring His children, made up of peoples from all nations, to His holy mountain and make them joyful in His house of prayer. He gathers the outcasts of Israel for the glory of His holy name.

When Jesus entered the temple and saw people buying and selling there, He was so angry that He overturned the tables of money changers and seats of those who sold doves and quoted Isaiah 56:7 as He did so (Matt. 21:13). A little while later He told the parable of the wedding feast in which we learn the same truths we learn here in Isaiah

56. The Lord opens wide His invitation to the wedding feast to those on the main roads (Gentiles) because the initial guests (Israel) were not responsive (Matt. 22:1–14). Throughout the book of Acts we learn of the spread of the gospel from the Jews to the Gentiles. It's the mission the Lord gave to His church, and we're to continue it today. Our greatest witness begins with our day of worship. Do we set aside Sunday for corporate worship with our brothers and sisters in Christ? During the week are we engaged in justice ministries in one way or another, at least by praying for them? Are we engaging with everyone the Lord places in our path, inviting them to church and sharing the reason for the hope we have within us?

II. The Lord Shepherds His People (56:9–57:21)

Israel's leaders were supposed to be godly, wise, righteous, and just, like tender shepherds, but instead they were self-centered, power hungry, ignorant, and drunk (Isa. 56:9–12). When leadership is unrighteous, the majority of the followers are often unrighteous. This certainly proved to be the case in Israel. The righteous ones were few and far between while idolaters were everywhere (57:1–13). Israel was playing the adulteress in her relationship with the Lord. The people had left Him to serve the gods of the nations, sacrificing their children and engaging in sexual sin. They found that life in idolatry, which strengthened them for the moment, was ultimately their downfall. In contrast, the righteous man who found refuge in the Lord remained strong because he became weak in humility (57:14–21). It is not that he was perfect, but he humbled himself before the Lord, acknowledging his sin. A person who practices such humble repentance experiences healing and restoration so that her lips can bear the fruit of praise to the Lord.

Jesus leaves us with two options just like this section of Isaiah does—peace or no peace. There is peace for those in Christ, and there is no peace for the wicked. Christ "Himself is our peace" (Eph. 2:14). He has reconciled both Jews and Gentiles "to God in one body through the cross" (v. 16). To those who look to Him in faith He says, "My peace I give to you" (John 14:27). He is the chief Shepherd who is wise and turned toward His Father's ways. He died so that God's people might gain life, pouring Himself out as a living drink offering. But to those who refuse to take up their cross and follow Him, He will bring a sword (Matt. 10:34–39; Rev. 19:15–16). You and I must choose whether we are going to swim upstream in our culture and stand for righteousness, finding true peace and rest, or whether we are going to bow down to the gods of our culture—money, power, popularity, fitness, entertainment, career, or sports. We have to decide whether we are going to be proud and self-centered or humble and God-centered. We must choose whether we are going to be tossed around by the stormy seas of wickedness or turn to Christ and rest in His peace. If we choose Christ, then our lips should never cease to sing His praise.

III. The Lord Saves His People (58:1–59:13)

It would be terrible to believe that your worship is pleasing to God only to find out it is not, or to think that your beliefs are sound only to learn that you have been told a lie. In this section of Isaiah we learn that God's people were filled with hypocrisy. They chose how they wanted to worship God instead of following how God wanted to be worshiped (Isa. 58:1–14). What they called acceptable was detestable to the Lord. They were pleasure seekers instead of God seekers and oppressors instead of helpers. The Lord wanted His people to love Him and to love their neighbor. When they took care of the needy in the name of the Lord, He would hear their prayers, but if they called to Him in wickedness, He would not. If they delighted in the Sabbath, then they would find delight in the Lord, but if they delighted in their own pleasures on His day, they would not.

The problem was never with the Lord's inability to hear or to save; it was always with Israel (Isa. 59:1–13). Their sins had separated them from God. From their hearts that conceived evil, to their heads that plotted evil, to their hands that carried out evil, Israel no longer knew the way of peace, righteousness, and justice. In the words of Jesus, "Men loved darkness rather than light, because their deeds were evil. For everyone practicing evil hates the light and does not come to the light, lest his deeds should be exposed" (John 3:19–20). Darkness had overtaken them (John 12:35). Those who walk in darkness and say that they have fellowship with God are lying because darkness can't coexist with light (1 John 1:6).

This section leaves us hanging on the note of sin and misery. We will have to wait until the next lesson to hit the high note of redemption again. But for now we should linger in the plight of humankind. We are dead in our trespasses and sins. Apart from someone opening our blind eyes, we cannot and will not choose light. Apart from God's grace, we remain under His curse and wrath. There is no satisfaction and no delight in darkness. The separation our sins have made is too great for us to bridge. His face will remain hidden and His ears closed to those who walk in darkness and have no light from His Son.

It's hard to admit we're hypocrites, but the more we come to see the state of our hearts, the more we'll run to Jesus. His Spirit gives us the power to say no to hypocrisy and yes to true worship. The Father does not call us as daughters and then leave us to clean ourselves up. Instead, He sent His Son to be our Shepherd and Savior. This Christ became to us sanctification, and it is in His image that we are being renewed day after day.

Processing It Together...

1. What do we learn about God in Isaiah 56:1–59:13?

2. How does this reshape how we should view our present circumstances?

3. What do we learn about God's Son, Jesus Christ?

4. How should this impact our relationship with God and with others?

5. What do we learn about God's covenant with His people?

6. How are we to live in light of this?

7. How can we apply Isaiah 56:1–59:13 to our lives today and in the future?

8. How should we apply this passage in our churches?

9. Look back at "Putting It in Perspective" in your personal study questions. What did you find challenging or encouraging about this lesson?

10. Look back at "Principles and Points of Application." How has this lesson impacted your life?

The Covenant Keeper and Crimson Conqueror

Isaiah 59:14–63:6

Purpose ...

Head. What do I need to know from this passage in Scripture?

- The Lord God will raise up an individual to be both the Covenant Keeper, bringing salvation to His people, and the Crimson Conqueror, bringing judgment to His enemies.

Heart. How does what I learn from this passage affect my internal relationship with the Lord?

- I am a kingdom disciple who has received the light, beauty, and holiness of Christ.

Hands. How does what I learn from this passage translate into action for God's kingdom?

- I will pray for justice, righteousness, and truth to be implemented in our public squares.
- I will teach the next generation to love, trust, obey, and serve the Lord.
- I will share the gospel with those from other nations in my neighborhood, schools, or churches and pray for my unbelieving friends, neighbors, and coworkers.
- I will take the good news of Jesus to the poor, brokenhearted, prisoners, and those enslaved to sin.
- I will prioritize membership in a local church and commit to faithfully attend corporate worship, serve with the gifts God has given me, and give of my tithes and offerings.

- I will pray for my persecuted brothers and sisters to persevere in the faith, and for the salvation of those who persecute them.

Personal Study...

Pray. Ask that God will open up your heart and mind as you study His Word. This is His story of redemption that He has revealed to us, and the Holy Spirit is our teacher.

Ponder the Passage. Read Isaiah 59:14–63:6.

- *Point.* What is the point of this passage? How does this relate to the point of the entire book?

- *Persons.* Who are the main people involved in this passage? What characterizes them?

- *Persons of the Trinity.* Where do you see God the Father, God the Son, and God the Holy Spirit in this passage?

- *Puzzling Parts.* Are there any parts of the passage that you don't quite understand or that seem interesting or confusing?

Put It in Perspective.

- *Place in Scripture.* What is the original context of this text? What is the redemptive-historical context—what has or hasn't happened in redemptive history at this point in Scripture? How does this text connect to Christ?

The following questions will help you if you got stuck on any of the previous questions, and they will help you dig a little deeper into the text, putting it all into perspective.

1. **59:14–20.** (a) How do these verses describe the cause-effect relationship between the lack of truth and society slipping?

   (b) How has the Lord's own arm brought salvation (see Luke 2:25–35)?

   (c) How do these verses anticipate the final day of judgment (see Rev. 19:15–16)?

(d) What point is Paul making when he uses verse 20 in the context of Romans 11:25–28?

2. 59:21. (a) What do you learn about the new covenant from Jeremiah 31:31–34?

(b) How is this fulfilled (see Hebrews 8; 10:1–18)?

3. 60:1–22. (a) How are these verses a fulfillment of Isaiah 55:1?

(b) In these verses, what makes it clear that Isaiah is not just speaking of God's people returning from Babylon, but a gathering of people on a worldwide scale?

(c) How do these verses anticipate Christ (see John 1:14; 8:12)? How do they anticipate the spread of the gospel in the book of Acts? How do they anticipate the new heavens and the new earth (see Rev. 21:4, 23–26; 22:5)?

4. 61:1–9. (a) Who is the "Me" Isaiah speaks of here (see Luke 4:16–21)?

(b) How does verse 6 reflect Exodus 19:6 and anticipate the priesthood of all believers (see 1 Peter 2:9)?

(c) How does verse 8 refer to 59:21, as well as 54:10 and 55:3?

5. 61:10–62:12. (a) How do the following verses display that the Lord was faithful to His words in 62:6–7 before the first coming of Christ: Luke 1:5–6, 8–10, 38, 46–55, 67–79; 2:25–38?

(b) How have these verses already been fulfilled (see Matt. 21:1–11; Eph. 5:25–27; Heb. 12:22–24, for example), and how do they look for a consummate fulfillment (Rev. 19:6–9; 21:2)?

6. 63:1–6. (a) By Isaiah's day, how had Edom become synonymous with the enemy of God's people (see 2 Kings 8:20; 14:7, 10; Ps. 137:7; Obad. 10–14)?

(b) How do these verses anticipate Revelation 6:15–17; 14:17–20; 19:11–16?

7. Compare the four Servant Songs of chapters 42–53 with the four songs about the Messiah in chapters 59–63, and then briefly state how Christ fulfills both of them by what you learned in the questions above:

42:1–9	59:21	Fulfillment in Christ
49:1–13	61:1–3	Fulfillment in Christ
50:4–9	61:10–62:7	Fulfillment in Christ
52:13–53:12	63:1–6	Fulfillment in Christ

Principles and Points of Application

8. **59:14–21.** (a) Spend time in prayer for your country, asking that justice, righteousness, and truth will be implemented in the public squares.

(b) Since we are united to Christ, the one who has put on righteousness as a breastplate and conquered our enemies (sin, death, and Satan) for us, we are now called to put on Christ's armor to stand firm against Satan's schemes (see Eph. 6:10–20). How are you doing this?

(c) Why does verse 21 encourage you to spend your days teaching the next generation to love, trust, obey, and serve the Lord?

9. **60:1–22.** (a) Since Christ is the light of the world and we are united to Him, we are to let our light shine before men so that they can see our good works and glorify our Father in heaven (Matt. 5:16). How are you doing this, and how are you teaching those under your leadership to do this?

(b) How are you remembering the nations in your prayers? How are you going to the nations with the gospel? In many cases, the nations have come to us. How are you engaging with those from other nations in your neighborhood, schools, and churches to share the gospel?

(c) Why is it encouraging to you that the Lord displays His glory?

(d) What shame or darkness are you facing today? Memorize verse 19:

> The LORD will be to you an everlasting light,
> And your God your glory.

10. 61:1–9. (a) How are you taking the good news of Jesus to the poor, brokenhearted, prisoners, and slaves to sin?

(b) Since you are united to Christ, the final and perfect High Priest, you are part of the royal priesthood of believers. How do you live sacrificially with those around you in light of Christ's sacrifice? How are you eagerly reconciling with others because Christ reconciled you to God when you were still dead in sin? How seriously do you take intercessory prayer, crying out to God on behalf of your family, country, church, pastors, and unbelievers you know?

11. 61:10–62:12. (a) The Lord God rejoices over His church, so what are the implications of this for you and membership in a local church? How are you showing your commitment to Christ's church?

(b) How do these verses encourage you regarding evangelism and missions?

12. 63:1–6. These verses should encourage us on the one hand and sober us on the other hand. How do they encourage you as you face rejection or persecution from unbelievers? How do they sober you as you think about your lost family members, friends, and neighbors? Spend time in prayer for the persecuted church, praying for their perseverance, as well as the salvation of those who persecute them. Pray also for your unbelieving friends, neighbors, and coworkers.

Putting It All Together…

What motivates your missions mindset? When you engage with non-Christians about the faith, why are you concerned to tell them the gospel and pray for the Lord to save them? One answer is that Christ told us to go and make disciples of all nations. And this is a very good answer! But another answer, and one I hope you incorporate into your thinking, is that the day of judgment is coming when the Lord will trample God's enemies. Today is the day of salvation, and the day of God's vengeance should motivate us to tell others about the only Savior, Jesus Christ. In this lesson we learn about the Covenant

Keeper and the Crimson Conqueror. The Lord God keeps His covenant with His people, raising up the Covenant Keeper, Jesus Christ, to obey the law perfectly on Israel's behalf and to take the wrath of God in their place. The Lord God also raises up Christ as the Crimson Conqueror, trampling His enemies according to His glorious justice.

I. The Covenant Keeper (59:14–60:22)

Israel had become blind in their sin (Isa. 59:14–15). Therefore, justice and righteousness were far from them, and truth was no longer paramount in the public squares. Truth was lacking among the people of truth! God's covenant people, who were supposed to be filled with truth so that all nations could be blessed through them, had failed to uphold God's justice and righteousness. Isaiah's contemporaries, who had heard of the exile of the Northern Kingdom at the hand of the Assyrians, had themselves been threatened by the Assyrians, and had heard that they would be exiled at the hand of the Babylonians, would have surely wondered if there was a future for God's people.

Into the darkness Isaiah spoke a shining ray of hope (Isa. 59:16–20). The Lord would bring salvation. He would put on righteousness and redemption and repay wickedness. He would be the Savior because no man was found to intercede. From generation to generation, the Lord would uphold His covenant faithfulness. He would put His Spirit on His people and His word in their mouths so that there would never cease to be a people to praise Him.

There is one man, the God-man, who always lives to intercede for God's people as the Covenant Keeper. He "became for us wisdom from God—and righteousness and sanctification and redemption" (1 Cor. 1:30). Because Christ put on righteousness as a breastplate and a helmet of salvation, we are united to Him in faith and are therefore to put on the full armor of God so that we might be able to stand against Satan's schemes. We are to marinate in God's truth daily. We are to recall the righteousness He has achieved for us and live rightly in light of it. We must remember the gospel and live from it every day of our lives. We need to rest in the salvation we've been given and engage in battle against sin because of it. And we need to use Scripture to counter the lies we're so prone to believe. Our Redeemer has already come, and we have come to Mount Zion, the city of the living God (Heb. 12:22). But He is coming again to rule the nations with a rod of iron (Rev. 19:15). This should fuel us toward the faithful proclamation of God's truth, whether in the public square or the privacy of our own home. We must not cease to declare the praises of our Redeemer to the next generation, urging them to follow truth and faithfully uphold it wherever God places them.

Just as there are four Servant Songs in chapters 42–53 that ultimately point to Jesus, so too there are four songs in chapters 59–63 that point to Jesus, the Messiah (59:21; 61:1–3; 61:10–62:7; 63:1–6). Each song is followed by verses that speak of God's people in God's place living with God's presence underneath God's precepts. You could say that the song of the King is first and the postlude about the kingdom is second. So

60:1–22 speaks of God's people. And we immediately learn they are a people of light. This light comes to them from the Lord and illumines their darkness with His glory. The light will be so great that nations will be drawn to it. The promise God gave to Abraham, "and in you all the families of the earth shall be blessed" (Gen. 12:3), would be fulfilled. The nations would come to Israel, redeemed by the Lord and reflecting His glory. The diversity of the nations brings even greater glory to God's already glorified house. Since the Lord's light has drawn these sons and daughters from every nation, they confess only the name of the Lord their God. Far from an "all roads lead to heaven" theology, Isaiah makes it clear that one must call upon the name of the Holy One of Israel to be saved. How glorious this truth must have been for Isaiah's contemporaries. Beyond exile was beauty and security. Salvation and praise would fill the streets; security and peace would surround them. The everlasting light of the Lord would fill the city of the Lord. His glory would shine through His glorified people.

Jesus told a parable about the kingdom of heaven, comparing it to a grain of mustard seed (the smallest of all seeds) that a man sowed in his field. It grew into a tree that was so big the birds came and made nests in its branches. This parable fits with what we have just learned in Isaiah. The Lord takes the smallest nation and makes it a mighty one in His own time. He is the light of the world that came revealing God's glory. He broke down the dividing wall of hostility between Jews and Gentiles, making one new man instead of two. He gave up the glory of heaven to come to earth and glorify God's people. Because Christ has shone His light on us, we are to walk in purity and wisdom as children of light (Eph. 5:8–15).

The second song of the King is found in 61:1–3. It's the King's own testimony. The Lord has anointed Him with His Spirit to bring both salvation for God's people and judgment for the wicked, the former to the praise of His glorious grace and the latter to the praise of His glorious justice.

On the Sabbath, Jesus used these verses in His hometown of Nazareth in the synagogue to tell His listeners that He was the fulfillment of them. He confronted His listeners with their hard-heartedness by telling them two examples of the Lord sending His prophets to speak to Gentiles because of Israel's rebelliousness (Luke 4:16–30). This highlights the context in Isaiah of the worldwide gathering of God's people, which is exactly what follows in 61:4–9. Foreigners (Gentiles) would be included among God's people who were set free to rebuild and restore. The redeemed would be released from shame and secure in the everlasting covenant. So too we are secure in the everlasting covenant and are priests of the Lord. Peter picks up the language God reserved for Israel and applies it to the New Testament church (Ex. 19:6; 1 Peter 2:9). Since we are a royal priesthood, we are to proclaim God's merciful work of calling us out of darkness into His marvelous light.

The third song of the King (61:10–62:7) is also the King's own testimony. Clothed with salvation and covered with righteousness, the bridegroom will make His bride beautiful and bring righteousness and praise to Zion. The Lord will give His people a new name and crown them with beauty. He will take delight in His covenant people, rejoicing over them as a bridegroom sings over his bride. He will establish Jerusalem so that others will see it and rejoice at what God has done. No longer will enemies invade the land. The Holy One of Israel will put His holy people, redeemed of the Lord, in His chosen city, never to be forsaken again.

Christ loved His church so much that He gave Himself up for her by humbling Himself and taking on the form of a servant, dying for her on the cross. In this way He saves and sanctifies His church so that He can present her to Himself in holiness and splendor. He nourishes and cherishes His church and is coming again to take her to spend an eternity with Him in the new heavens and the new earth. The marriage supper of the Lamb awaits us, where we will behold the face of our beloved bridegroom, Jesus Christ. He has sought us and bought us so that we can be a people holy for Him. We should never cease to cry out to Him, recalling His promises, believing them, and praying He will come quickly to consummate His kingdom. In the meantime, let us proclaim to the ends of the earth that salvation is in Christ alone.

II. The Crimson Conqueror (63:1–6)

The fourth and final song of the King (63:1–6) speaks of the mighty Savior. He comes from Edom, which in Scripture is proverbial for God's enemies (see, for example, 2 Kings 8:20; 14:7, 10; Obad. 10–14). Appropriately, Edom means "red," and Bozrah means "vintage." The names fit with the imagery of blood and winepress. This mighty Savior trod God's enemies alone. The day of vengeance had come, and there was no arm but His to bring Him salvation. His own anger upheld Him as He trampled the wicked in wrath. Isaiah's contemporaries should have shuddered as they heard of the Crimson Conqueror. They needed to reckon with the day of vengeance. Whose side were they on—the Lord's or the enemy's?

Christ came the first time to redeem and restore God's people. But He is coming again as the Crimson Conqueror. In righteousness He will judge and declare war. In a robe dipped in blood, He will return with the armies of heaven to strike down the nations and rule them with a rod of iron. The King of kings and Lord of lords will tread the winepress of the fury of God's wrath (Rev. 19:11–16). Whose side are you on? Only those who have placed their faith in Christ will escape the fury of God's wrath. This should motivate us to examine our hearts and to boldly proclaim to all those we come into contact with that salvation is found in no one else except Jesus. Let us look to Him, the Covenant Keeper and the Crimson Conqueror, in praise and adoration and live in such a way that displays we believe Jesus is coming again to judge the living and the dead.

The Crimson Conqueror should motivate your missions. Look around you at the non-Christians you know and understand that if they're not united with Christ, they will endure the fury of His wrath on the day of vengeance. Today is the time to tell them about the gospel. Pray for the Lord to give you the opportunity and then speak boldly and kindly to them.

Processing It Together...

1. What do we learn about God in Isaiah 59:14–63:6?

2. How does this reshape how we should view our present circumstances?

3. What do we learn about God's Son, Jesus Christ?

4. How should this impact our relationship with God and with others?

5. What do we learn about God's covenant with His people?

6. How are we to live in light of this?

7. How can we apply Isaiah 59:14–63:6 to our lives today and in the future?

8. How should we apply this passage in our churches?

9. Look back at "Putting It in Perspective" in your personal study questions. What did you find challenging or encouraging about this lesson?

10. Look back at "Principles and Points of Application." How has this lesson impacted your life?

A Praying People and a Promise-Keeping God

Isaiah 63:7–66:24

Purpose...

Head. What do I need to know from this passage in Scripture?

- God's people pray because God is faithful to keep His promises.

Heart. How does what I learn from this passage affect my internal relationship with the Lord?

- I am a kingdom disciple who can confidently pray because Jesus is my Great High Priest.

Hands. How does what I learn from this passage translate into action for God's kingdom?

- I will pray for my family, friends, neighbors, and coworkers who remain in unbelief, asking the Lord to open their eyes to their sinfulness and save them.
- I will encourage others to live in holiness by God's power.
- I will join with others to worship God in reverence and awe.
- I will rely on the Lord's strength and power to proclaim the gospel to every nation.

Personal Study...

Pray. Ask that God will open up your heart and mind as you study His Word. This is His story of redemption that He has revealed to us, and the Holy Spirit is our teacher.

Ponder the Passage. Read Isaiah 63:7–66:24.

- *Point.* What is the point of this passage? How does this relate to the point of the entire book?

- *Persons.* Who are the main people involved in this passage? What characterizes them?

- *Persons of the Trinity.* Where do you see God the Father, God the Son, and God the Holy Spirit in this passage?

- *Puzzling Parts.* Are there any parts of the passage that you don't quite understand or that seem interesting or confusing?

Put It in Perspective.

- *Place in Scripture.* What is the original context of this text? What is the redemptive-historical context—what has or hasn't happened in redemptive history at this point in Scripture? How does this text connect to Christ?

The following questions will help you if you got stuck on any of the previous questions, and they will help you dig a little deeper into the text, putting it all into perspective.

1. **63:7–14.** (a) What do you learn from Exodus 14:1–17:7 that provides important background for these verses?

(b) These verses form a foundation for the prayer in 63:15–64:12. Why are they so critical for Isaiah and his contemporaries as they walked in the days of darkness between the Northern Kingdom's exile to Assyria and the Southern Kingdom's exile to Babylon?

(c) These verses make clear that the Holy Spirit was leading God's people and giving them rest. According to 1 Corinthians 10:1–5, who followed them?

(d) According to Hebrews 3:1–6, how is Jesus greater than Moses?

2. 63:15–64:3. (a) How do Exodus 14:3; 15:11; Numbers 10:33; Deuteronomy 4:25–26; 26:15; 32:6; Joshua 2:8–10 provide background for these verses?

(b) Who are the servants in 63:17 (see 10:20–22)?

(c) How has Christ answered the plea for mercy in this prayer (see Matt. 27:51–54)? How will this consummately be fulfilled (see Heb. 12:26–27; Rev. 6:12–17)?

3. 64:4–5. (a) According to these verses, what does God do for those who wait for Him, joyfully work righteousness, and remember Him in His ways?

(b) According to Acts 2:37–39 and 3:19–21, how can someone be in their sins for a long time and still be saved?

4. 64:6–12. (a) As Isaiah looks ahead to the Babylonian exile, what does he say prophetically, as though it has already happened?

(b) What is the point Paul is making when he uses the imagery of the potter and the clay (v. 8) in Romans 9:20–29?

(c) How are verses 9–12 ultimately answered (see John 1:14–18; 2:19–22; Acts 7:47–53)?

5. 65:1–7. (a) How does verse 1 reflect Genesis 12:3, and how does Paul use verses 1–2 in the context of Romans 10:14–21?

(b) How did the Lord respond to the Israel of Isaiah's day, and why (see Ex. 20:4–5; Deut. 4:15–28)?

(c) How does verse 1 anticipate the spread of the gospel to the Gentiles in the book of Acts? Note a couple of specific examples.

(d) What does the New Testament say about idolatry (see, for example, 1 Cor. 10:14–22)?

6. **65:8–12.** (a) Why is it significant that "My servants" is used synonymously with "My people"?

(b) What other time in Israel's history did the Lord not destroy an entire city for the sake of one of His servants (see Gen. 19:18–22)?

(c) How does verse 9 reflect Genesis 3:15; 15:5; 22:17–18?

(d) How do these verses anticipate the final day of judgment (see Matt. 25:31–46)?

7. **65:13–25.** (a) How do verses 13–14 reflect the covenant blessings found in Deuteronomy 28:8–12 and curses found in Deuteronomy 28:17, 25–26, 37, 45–48?

(b) How do verses 15–16 reflect Genesis 17:5–8?

(c) What is Isaiah's point in using metaphorical language in verse 20? How do we know from other passages of Scripture that there won't be any death or sinners in the new creation?

(d) How do verses 21–25 anticipate the reversal of the curse in Genesis 3:14–19 and Deuteronomy 28:30, 40–41?

(e) How do these verses anticipate 2 Peter 3:13 and Revelation 21:1–4?

8. **66:1–14.** (a) How does verse 1 look back to 1 Kings 8:27 and forward to Acts 7:47–50; 17:24–25?

(b) How does verse 2 reflect David's prayer in 1 Chronicles 29:14–19?

(c) How do verses 10–14 reveal God's faithfulness to His promises regarding Jerusalem and His people and fulfill His offer of comfort in 40:1–2?

(d) How do these verses anticipate Hebrews 12:22–24?

9. **66:15–21.** (a) What is the end for apostate Israel, and how do these verses both reflect the sword and fire in Genesis 3:24 and anticipate Hebrews 12:25, 29 and Revelation 19:12, 15?

(b) How do these verses display the Lord as the ultimate evangelist and missionary and anticipate John 11:52 and Ephesians 2:11–22?

(c) How does verse 21 reflect Exodus 19:6 and anticipate 1 Peter 2:9 and Revelation 1:6?

10. **66:22–24.** (a) How are these verses a fitting conclusion to the entire book? (You may want to skim the introductory material in 1:1–5:30.)

(b) How does verse 24 anticipate Jesus's words in Mark 9:43–48, as well as in Revelation 21:8?

Principles and Points of Application

11. **63:7–14.** (a) In your life, what tempts you to harden your heart in your sin or suffering instead of believing God's promises and looking to Him in faith?

(b) Spend time in prayer for family, friends, neighbors, and coworkers who remain in unbelief, asking the Lord to open their eyes to their sinfulness and save them.

12. **63:15–64:12.** (a) Are you quick to recognize that all your righteous deeds are like a polluted garment apart from Christ, or do you often try to impress God with your works to earn His favor? Explain your answer.

(b) As those who are united to Christ, we can rest assured that our Father is no longer angry with us. Write out a prayer of thanksgiving.

(c) As believers who have received God's mercy, we are to renounce ungodliness and live in holiness by God's power. How does your life display God's mercy and the light of the gospel (see 2 Cor. 4:1–12)?

13. 65:1–66:24. (a) Since we are eagerly awaiting the new creation, we are to be pure and at peace with others (2 Peter 3:14). In what areas of your life do you need to grow in purity? In what areas do you need to be a peacemaker?

(b) Since we have already come to the heavenly Jerusalem, how do we display our gratefulness to God (Heb. 12:22–24, 28)?

(c) Since the Lord is the ultimate evangelist and missionary, how are you relying on His strength and power to proclaim the good news of Jesus Christ to every nation? Spend time in prayer, asking the Lord to open more opportunities for you to do so.

(d) The book of Isaiah has painted a breathtaking picture of the gospel of Jesus Christ according to Old Testament prophecy. Often we want to just teach about the new creation and leave out the doctrine of hell. But Isaiah makes it clear that we must teach both. How does the doctrine of hell motivate you to participate in evangelism and missions?

Putting It All Together...

If someone asked you to tell the story of the Bible in four words, a good answer would be "creation, fall, redemption and consummation." You could show them the major ups and downs of this story from Genesis to Revelation. Or you could show them Isaiah 63:7–66:24. At the end of this glorious book, we find the biblical story in a nutshell. God is set forth as the Creator King who sits on His heavenly throne, with earth as His footstool. He is the Father and potter of His people. Israel is set forth as the rebellious one who refused to hear His voice and fell into idolatry. The remnant of Israel is set forth as the redeemed people of God who have humble hearts. And God's holy city, the New Jerusalem, is set forth as the consummated kingdom, where God will dwell with His people forever in peace, joy, and gladness, with no suffering, sin, death, or shame.

I. A Praying People (63:7–64:12)

We learn from 63:7–14 that the prayer of the redeemed (63:15–64:12) is rooted in God's covenant love, which is rich with compassion and steadfastness. Since God cannot ultimately forsake His children, He becomes their Savior and Redeemer. Though in rebellion they grieved the Holy Spirit of God so that He became their enemy, He ultimately led them through the exodus for the sake of His glorious name. As the remnant recalled God's past redemption, they gained courage in the present and hope for the future.

In 62:6–7 we read,

> I have set watchmen on your walls, O Jerusalem;
> They shall never hold their peace day or night.
> You who make mention of the LORD, do not keep silent,
> And give Him no rest till He establishes
> And till He makes Jerusalem a praise in the earth.

The prayer in 63:15–64:12 implores the Lord to make Jerusalem a praise in the earth:

> Look down from heaven,
> And see....
> Doubtless You are our Father....
>
> Oh, that You would rend the heavens!
> That You would come down!...
>
> Our holy and beautiful temple...
> Is burned up with fire....
> Will You restrain Yourself because of these things, O LORD?
>   (63:15–16; 64:1, 11–12)

The remnant of God's people looked to Him as Father when the majority of those descended from Father Abraham wanted nothing to do with them. As His servants, they remembered His kingship and longed for its return. They called for their King to come down in power to be with them, longing for the nations to know that His name is above every other name. Their confidence that He will come is rooted in His covenant promises. As the redeemed remnant, they confessed their sins and the sins of the nation, and they knew salvation would be an act of mercy and grace. Like Isaiah, they knew they were a people of unclean lips, for they had seen the King, the Lord of hosts (Isa. 6:5). Yet the remnant asked their Redeemer to look on them as the work of His hand and not keep silent. Surely their hope was that of Isaiah—their sin would be atoned for and their guilt taken away by someone other than themselves.

Christ came to God's people and became their Savior. In all their affliction, He was afflicted. In His love and pity, He redeemed them. He is the superior Moses who has led His people through a greater exodus—the exodus from sin, death, and shame into a life of freedom in Him. He is the Good Shepherd who has laid down His life for the sheep by the blood of the eternal covenant. He not only looked down from heaven and saw God's people in distress but He came down from heaven in zeal and might and compassion to reveal our heavenly Father to us. The earth quaked on the day that He died on the cross and the curtain of the temple was torn in two from top to bottom to display He alone is the God who acts for those who wait for Him. Even while we were enemies, He reconciled us to our Father, so that we might be a people who proclaim His excellence and do the works that He has prepared beforehand for us to do. He has brought us to the New Jerusalem even now, where the blood of Christ cries grace and mercy. As the redeemed, we have the privilege to come before our heavenly Father through the blood of Christ and by the power of the Holy Spirit. Glory be to the Father who appointed our redemption, the Son who accomplished it, and the Holy Spirit who applies it! May we never cease to be a praying people who are filled with praise for the person and work of Jesus Christ.

II. A Promise-Keeping God (65:1–66:24)
Previously God's people asked (64:12),

> Will You restrain Yourself because of these things, O LORD?
> Will You hold Your peace, and afflict us very severely?

The Lord answered that He has not been silent but has been speaking (Isa. 65:1–7). He was speaking to Gentiles, calling them to salvation, and He was speaking to His rebellious people, pronouncing their judgment. But He was also speaking to His remnant, proclaiming His promises. The Lord had preserved the seed of the woman—Christ and His church (Gen. 3:15), through the time of Noah to Abraham to Moses to David to Isaiah, and He would continue to preserve it until His redemptive purposes were complete. For those who refused to listen to His words and answer His call, the sword of judgment would fall. The covenant blessings would come on His servants, but the covenant curses would come on His betrayers (Isa. 65:8–16). The God of truth would triumph over His enemies and bring blessing for His people.

This blessing would be nothing less than the new creation (Isa. 65:17–25). God's people, filled with joy and gladness, would no longer experience sin or death or suffering of any kind. Isaiah's metaphorical language here reminds us that the New Jerusalem will be more glorious than anything we can imagine; the biblical authors put it in terms of what we can understand. See verse 20, for example:

> No more shall an infant from there live but a few days,
> Nor an old man who has not fulfilled his days;
> For the child shall die one hundred years old,
> But the sinner being one hundred years old shall be accursed.

From other passages of Scripture we know that there will be no death or sin in the new heavens and the new earth (Rev. 21:4, 27), so what is Isaiah's point here? He's affirming that there will be no more death or sin by painting a picture we can understand. If it were even possible for death to be in the New Jerusalem, there wouldn't be the death of an infant or the premature death of an adult. Instead, they would live their full lives. Likewise, if it were possible for humankind to sin in the Holy City and reach one hundred years old, their sin would still be revealed and judged.[1] In the new heavens and the new earth the curse of Genesis 3:15 will be reversed. Relationships will be filled with kindness instead of conflict. Work will be filled with fruitfulness instead of futility. The creation will no longer groan but be glad. There will be perfect peace in God's paradise.

How then should Isaiah and his contemporaries live in light of such a future with the King on His heavenly throne for which earth is just a footstool? They were to humble themselves before Him and live according to His word and ways (Isa. 66:1–2). For those who would rebel, judgment would come (vv. 3–6). Their taunting and scoffing directed at the remnant would return on their own heads. The Lord God will not be put to shame.

The Lord's purposes for birthing Zion will be fulfilled (Isa. 66:7–14). Jerusalem will be filled with joyful delight. Nations will flow to her and within her. The comfort God promised His people (40:1) finds its perfect fulfillment in His place with His presence under His precepts.

But outside the city would be the fire of judgment (Isa. 66:15–24). Idolaters will meet the sword of the Lord. As the nations stream into God's city under God's banner with God's name, His glory will be revealed to the entire world to the praise of His glorious grace. On the other hand, as the rebellious reveled in their idolatry, so they would reap what they sowed in an eternity in hell to the praise of God's glorious justice.

It is Christ who is our peace and made Jews and Gentiles one so that the Lord God could be known by those who did not ask for Him. It is Christ who is the Servant, whose perfect work saved humankind from destruction. It is Christ who has become to us peace and joy and gladness. It is Christ who came as the true temple and tabernacled among us to reveal God's grace and truth. And it is Christ who, more often than anyone else in Scripture, spoke of the fire that will not be quenched. That the book of Isaiah ends on such a sobering note should give us pause. Sometimes it's not the glories of the new creation that will awaken our hearts to grace but the gruesomeness of hell. Perhaps the doctrine of hell should be on our lips more often than it is as we proclaim Christ to the nations. It should certainly motivate us to pray for our family, friends, and neighbors who stand in rebellion against Him, refusing to hear His word and walk in His ways.

❧ ◆ ◆ ◆

---

1. Motyer, *Prophecy of Isaiah*, 530.

You have the story of the Bible in a nutshell to share with your family, friends, and neighbors. Will you take what you've learned this week—indeed, what you've learned over this entire study—and share it with those who need to hear the good news of Jesus Christ? The Lord goes before you as the ultimate missionary and evangelist. All authority in heaven and earth has already been given to Him. He is always with us as we seek to make disciples of all nations. This will look different in the details for each of us, but in design it will be the same. For each of us, our worship is our greatest witness. Let us never cease to recount the Lord's lovingkindness and to yield to the Holy Spirit as we look to our heavenly Father and rejoice in our Redeemer.

Processing It Together...

1. What do we learn about God in Isaiah 63:7–66:24?

2. How does this reshape how we should view our present circumstances?

3. What do we learn about God's Son, Jesus Christ?

4. How should this impact our relationship with God and with others?

5. What do we learn about God's covenant with His people?

6. How are we to live in light of this?

7. How can we apply Isaiah 63:7–66:24 to our lives today and in the future?

8. How should we apply this passage in our churches?

9. Look back at "Putting It in Perspective" in your personal study questions. What did you find challenging or encouraging about this lesson?

10. Look back at "Principles and Points of Application." How has this lesson impacted your life?

Bibliography

The ESV Gospel Transformation Bible. Wheaton, Ill: Crossway, 2013.

The ESV Study Bible. Wheaton, Ill.: Crossway, 2008.

Johnson, Dennis E. *Him We Proclaim: Preaching Christ from All the Scriptures.* Phillipsburg, N.J.: P&R, 2007.

Motyer, J. Alec. *The Prophecy of Isaiah: An Introduction and Commentary.* Downers Grove, Ill.: IVP Academic, 1993.

Oswalt, John N. *The Book of Isaiah: Chapters 1–39.* The New International Commentary on the Old Testament. Grand Rapids: Eerdmans, 1986.

———. *The Book of Isaiah: Chapters 40–66.* The New International Commentary on the Old Testament. Grand Rapids: Eerdmans, 1986.

Robertson, O. Palmer. *The Christ of the Prophets.* Phillipsburg, N.J.: P&R, 2004.